2

Workbook

SECOND EDITION

Ken Beatty

HEINLE
CENGAGE Learning

Australia • Brazil • Japan • Korea • Mexico • Singapore • Spain • United Kingdom • United States

Go For It! Second Edition, Workbook 2
Ken Beatty

Publisher, Global ELT: Christopher Wenger

Editorial Manager: Bertha de Llano

Director of Product Development:
　Anita Raducanu

Development Editor: Rebecca Klevberg,
　Ivor Williams

Development Editor: Margarita Matte

Contributing Writers: John Chapman

Director of Marketing, ESL/ELT: Amy Mabley

International Marketing Manager:
　Eric Bredenberg

Senior Production Editor: Sally Cogliano

Senior Print Buyer: Mary Beth Hennebury

Project Manager: Kris Swanson

Interior Design / Composition:
Miguel Angel Contreras Perez; Israel Munoz Olmos

Illustrator: James Rivera Contreras

Photo Manager: Sheri Blaney

Photo Researcher: Melissa Goodrum

Cover Designer: Linda Beaupre

For product information and technology assistance, contact us at
Cengage Learning Customer & Sales Support, 1-800-354-9706

For permission to use material from this text or product,
submit all requests online at **cengage.com/permissions**
Further permissions questions can be emailed to
permissionrequest@cengage.com

ISBN-13: 978-1-4130-0021-4

ISBN-10: 1-4130-0021-5

Heinle
25 Thomson Place
Boston, MA 02210
USA

Cengage Learning is a leading provider of customized learning solutions with office locations around the globe, including Singapore, the United Kingdom, Australia, Mexico, Brazil, and Japan. Locate your local office at:
international.cengage.com/region

Cengage Learning products are represented in Canada by Nelson Education, Ltd.

Visit Heinle online at **elt.heinle.com**

Visit our corporate website at **cengage.com**

Photo Credits
3: BL: ©Thomson/Heinle; BR: ©Kevin Peterson/Photodisc Green/Getty; 8: ©Hemera Photo-Objects; 13: TL: ©Reuters New Media Inc./CORBIS; 13: TR: ©S.I.N./CORBIS; 16: ©Ross Anania/Getty; 17: ©Thomson/Heinle; 18: T&B ©Hemera Photo-Objects; 23: TR: © Thomson/Heinle; CL: © Thomson Heinle; CR: © Photodisc Collection/Getty; 27: TRH: ©Hemera Photo-Objects; TRC: ©Hemera Photo-Objects; TRD: ©Felicia Martinez/Photoedit; TRM: ©Hemera Photo-Objects; CH: ©Hemera Photo-Objects; CL: ©Felicia Martinez/Photoedit; 29: ©PhotoLink/Photodisc Green/Getty; 30, 31: ©Thomson/Heinle; 34: ©Ingo Jezierski/Photodisc/Getty; 35: TLs ©Photodisc Blue/Getty; 35: TC: ©PhotoLink/Getty; 35: TR: ©Photo 24/Brand X Pictures/Getty; 40: ©Photodisc Green/Getty; 41: ©ISrael Munoz; 43: ©Thomson/Heinle; 44: all: ©Hemera Photo-Objects; 53: © Thomson/Heinle; 61: ©LWA-Dann Tarrdif/CORBIS; 65: T: ©Richard Cummins/SuperStock; 65: C: ©Joanna McCarthy/SuperStock; 65: B: ©Jeff Greenberg/Index Stock Imagery; 69: ©Gunter Marx Photography/CORBIS

Printed in the United States of America
11 12 13 14 15　20 19 18 17 16

Table of Contents

Unit 1 LESSON A
This is my friend Mika.

1 Unscramble the words to complete the chart.

zibarl
succo
daalnhit
mabolcoi
askao
hisaganh

Countries	Cities
Brazil	_____
_____	_____
_____	_____

2 Circle the correct word.

1. A: Hi, Judy. ((Is) / Are) this your friend?
   B: Yes. (This / These) is Mei.
2. A: Where (is / are) Yuka from?
   B: (I'm / She's) from Japan.
3. A: (Do / Does) you live in Sao Paulo?
   B: No, I (don't / doesn't).
4. A: Where (are / does) Erica live?
   B: She (live / lives) in Puebla.
5. A: (Is / Are) you from Peru?
   B: No, (he's / we're) not.

3 Fill in the blanks. Then number the sentences 1 to 7 to make a conversation.

I'm   don't   where   do   is   not   what's

GFI Go for it!

Chat   *on line*

____ ___ from Italy.

1 Hi. I'm Kim. __What's__ your name?

____ Italy? _____ you live in Rome?

____ _____ are you from, John?

____ Hello, Kim. My name _____ John.

____ No, I _____. I live in Venice. Are you from Italy, too?

____ No, I'm _____. I'm from South Korea.

Message [_____] Send

4 Match the sentences to the responses.

1. Are you from Colombia?	_c_	a. My friend Lee.
2. Do you live in Mexico City?	____	b. They're from Italy.
3. Where are you from?	____	c. Yes, I am.
4. Hi, my name's Yuko.	____	d. No, she's not. She's from Brazil.
5. Who's that?	____	e. No, I don't.
6. Where are your friends from?	____	f. Hi. My name's Roberto.
7. Is your teacher from the U.S.?	____	g. We're from Thailand.

5 Unscramble the questions. Then answer with your own information.

1. (name / what's / teacher's / your)
   Q: _What's your teacher's name?_____
   A: _____

2. (you / from / are / where)
   Q: _____
   A: _____

3. (friend / where / best / live / does / your)
   Q: _____
   A: _____

4. (United / your / are / classmates / the / from / States)
   Q: _____
   A: _____

6 Read about two students and fill in the chart. Then add your own information.

GFI Go for it!
Chat   on line

Hi! My name is Lydia Burgos. I'm an exchange student. I'm from Mexico. Now I live in Tokyo, Japan. I really like the food in Japan. The sushi is great!

Message [   ] Send

GFI Go for it!
Chat   on line

Hello. My name is Young-ho Park. I'm from South Korea. I live in Seoul. I like soccer and baseball.

Message [   ] Send

Name	From . . .	Lives in . . .	Likes . . .
Lydia Burgos			

LESSON B What nationality are you?

7 Look at the picture. Write two sentences about each person.

1. ___Sun-hee is from Korea. She's South Korean.___

2. _____

3. _____

4. _____

8 Where are your favorite stars from? What nationalities are they? Complete the chart for three stars you like. Then write about them.

Name	Country	City	Nationality
Shakira	Colombia	Barranquilla	Colombian

My favorite singer is Shakira. She's from . . .

_____

_____

_____

_____

_____

Go for it!
Using a map

Look at the map. Then write the correct letter next to each country below.

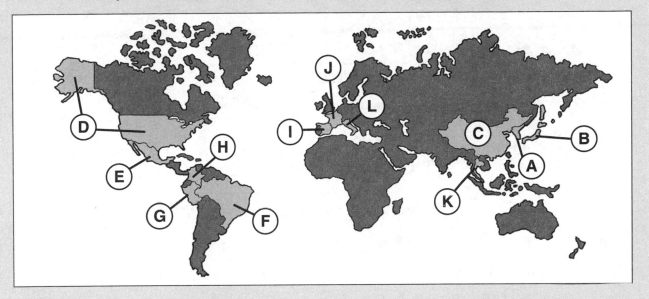

1. Brazil	_f_	5. Italy	____	9. Peru	____
2. China	____	6. Japan	____	10. Spain	____
3. Colombia	____	7. South Korea	____	11. Thailand	____
4. France	____	8. Mexico	____	12. the United States	____

Look at the chart. Write the names of the countries from largest to smallest population.
Smallest population

Population Chart 2003

Country	Population (in millions)
South Korea	48
Peru	28
Italy	58
Brazil	176
China	1,289
France	60
Colombia	41
Japan	128
Mexico	105
Thailand	63
Spain	40
USA	292

Largest population

1. _China_
2. _____
3. _____
4. _____
5. _____
6. _____
7. _____
8. _____
9. _____
10. _____
11. _____
12. _____

Smallest population

Unit 2

I'd like a large pizza, please.

1 Find these words.

olives

tomatoes

onions

shrimp

pineapple

sausage

ham

green peppers

cheese

mushrooms

```
B  H  A  W  X  A  D  S  H  R  I  M  P  L  T
B  A  H  I  S  I  B  R  I  S  A  A  R  G  T
O  M  S  A  O  L  I  V  E  S  A  C  D  R  O
A  I  I  B  N  I  B  A  A  M  O  A  A  E  M
A  P  C  A  I  B  O  B  H  A  Q  C  S  E  A
B  E  I  A  O  I  I  I  A  L  I  H  Y  N  T
Z  Z  H  C  N  I  A  D  I  A  I  E  A  P  O
K  P  F  I  S  W  A  I  C  C  I  E  A  E  E
G  E  F  I  W  A  B  E  I  G  L  S  A  P  S
I  R  R  G  A  I  S  I  I  A  A  E  C  P  A
B  S  S  A  U  S  A  G  E  A  A  S  I  E  I
J  M  U  S  H  R  O  O  M  S  B  I  C  R  A
I  P  C  H  W  A  M  A  R  I  C  A  I  S  A
K  C  P  I  N  E  A  P  P  L  E  H  A  A  I
```

2 Circle the correct words. Then match the questions to the answers.

1. Would Alice (like / likes) onions? __a__

2. What would your brother (likes / like)? _____

3. What (kind / size) of toppings would you like? _____

4. What (kind / size) pizza would you like? _____

5. (What / What's) your address? _____

6. Would Steve and Dave (likes / like) ham? _____

a. Yes, she would.

b. No. They'd like shrimp.

c. I'd like onion and tomatoes.

d. He'd like a cheese pizza.

e. I'd like a large pizza.

f. It's 16 Stone Street.

3 Fill in the blanks. Then number the sentences to make a conversation.

would	I'd	what	it's	like	please	what's	hello

____ Hi. I'd _____ a pizza, please.

____ _____ like sausage.

____ A small one, _____ .

____ That's one small sausage pizza. _____ your address?

_1_ _Hello_ , Marco's Pizza.

____ What toppings _____ you like?

____ Okay. One sausage pizza. _____ size would you like?

____ _____ 610 Main Street.

4 Write the questions.

1. Q: _What would you like?_____

   A: I'd like a pizza, please.

2. Q: _____

   A: They'd like a large pizza.

3. Q: _____

   A: Yes, we would. We love onions.

4. Q: _____

   A: Jerry would like tomatoes, cheese, and shrimp.

5. Q: _____

   A: No, thanks. I don't like ham.

5 What kind of pizza would you like? Complete the order form with your information. Then draw your pizza.

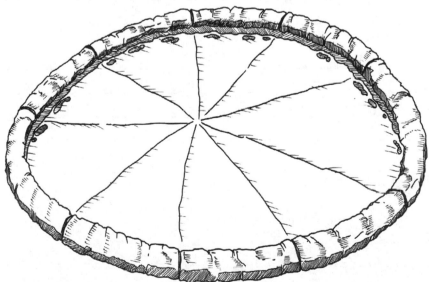

PIZZA To Go
"Best pizza in town"

Name: _____

Address: _____
_____

Telephone: _____

Size: ☐ small ☐ medium ☐ large

Toppings:
☐ olives ☐ shrimp ☐ sausage
☐ mushrooms ☐ ham ☐ onions

Total: $ _____

LESSON B How much is the special?

6 Fill in the missing letters to complete the menu.

Joe's Diner

Drinks

m i l k	$1.25
s _ _ a	$1.00

Food

s a _ d _ i c _	$4.40
h _ t d o _	$2.70
_ i z _ a	$7.90
s _ a g _ e _ t i	$5.35
s _ l _ d	$1.50
a _ p _ e	$ .80
f _ e n _ h f _ i _ s	$ .75
_ c e - c r _ _ m c o _ e	$1.45

7 Use the cues to complete the conversations. Then place an order for yourself. Remember to use a, an, or some.

1. Waitress: (What / like) _What would you like?_____

   Jane: (hot dog) _____

   Waitress: (Would / like / french fries?) _____

   Jane: (no / like / salad) _____

2. Waiter: (What / like) _____

   Kevin: (We / large / cheese / pizza) _____

   Waiter: (Would / like / something to drink?) _____

   Maria: (yes / two sodas) _____

3. Waiter: (What / like) _____

   You: _____

   Waiter: (Would / like / something to drink?) _____

   You: _____

8 How much are the meals? Write the amounts below.

1. Jane: _____

2. Kevin and Maria: _____

3. You: _____

8   EATING OUT

9 Read the paragraph and circle the toppings you find. Then answer the questions.

Hi Mom!
We all want pizza at the party tonight!
Anna would like a small pizza with tomatoes, mushrooms, and onions. Lee would like a small pizza too. He'd like olives, tomatoes, cheese, and ham. John and Sara would like a medium pizza with cheese, tomatoes, and green peppers. Carlos and I would like a large pizza with ham, mushrooms, and green peppers.
Thanks!
Jim

Waldo's Pizza!
Toppings:
onions, cheese, tomatoes, ham, mushrooms, and green peppers

Prices:
Small - $8.50
Med. - $12.25
Large - $16.75

1. How many pizzas would Jim and his friends like? <u>They'd like four pizzas.</u>
2. What sizes would they like? _____
3. Would John and Sara like a small pizza? _____
4. Which pizza topping on Lee's order is not on the menu? _____
5. Would Lee like onions? _____
6. What would Jim like? _____
7. How much is the pizza order for the party? _____

Go for it!
Unhealthy foods

Some foods are high in fat and calories. Look at the chart and choose a healthy meal. Circle a sandwich, drink, and dessert with less than 450 calories and 35 grams of fat.

		Calories	Fat (grams)
Sandwiches	hamburger	450	35
	hot dog	190	15
	turkey sandwich	215	5
Drinks	orange juice	122	0.2
	milk	150	8.2
	soda	190	0
Desserts	ice cream	270	14.3
	apple	80	0.8
	big cookie	100	4.5

Now, write about the fat and calories your meal has.

_____

_____

_____

Unit 3 LESSON A
Where's the rock concert?

1 Unscramble the kinds of music. Then complete the chart below.

1. opp   pop
2. chotne
3. lisscalca
4. lassa
5. garege
6. noutcry
7. kroc
8. pra

Music I like...

Music I don't like...

2 Number the sentences to make a conversation.

___ Are the rap CDs between the salsa and rock CDs?

___ Thank you.

___ No, they're not. They're behind the pop.

___ Turn right and go straight. It's next to the rap CDs.

_1_ Can I help you?

___ Yes, please. Where's the techno music?

3 Fill in the blanks to complete the CD and video shop advertisement. Use the words in the box.

| right | next to | across from | behind | left | between | straight |

Welcome to the Big Fun music and video store!

For our pop music section, turn ___left___. The salsa music is _____ the pop music. And _____ the salsa music is our rock music section. Our new rap music section is _____ the rock. And yes, we have country music! It's to the _____ of the door. We also have videos! Go _____ and turn left for our international videos in Spanish and Italian. The sports videos are _____ the language videos and our cool new music videos. You'll love Big Fun!

4 Complete the questions with **is** or **are**. Then match the questions to the answers.

1. Where _is_ the new Ronaldo video? _f_
2. ____ the music videos near the sports ones? ___
3. ____ Jet Li from Japan? ___
4. Where ____ the Spanish videos? ___
5. What nationality ____ Zinedine Zidane? ___
6. Where ____ Salma Hayek from? ___

a. They're next to the Italian ones.
b. She's from Mexico.
c. He's French.
d. Yes, they are.
e. No, he's not. He's from China.
f. It's in the sports section.

LESSON B What do you think about rap?

5 Read the cartoon and fill in the blanks.

they're   are   do   is   think   she's   like   don't   it's

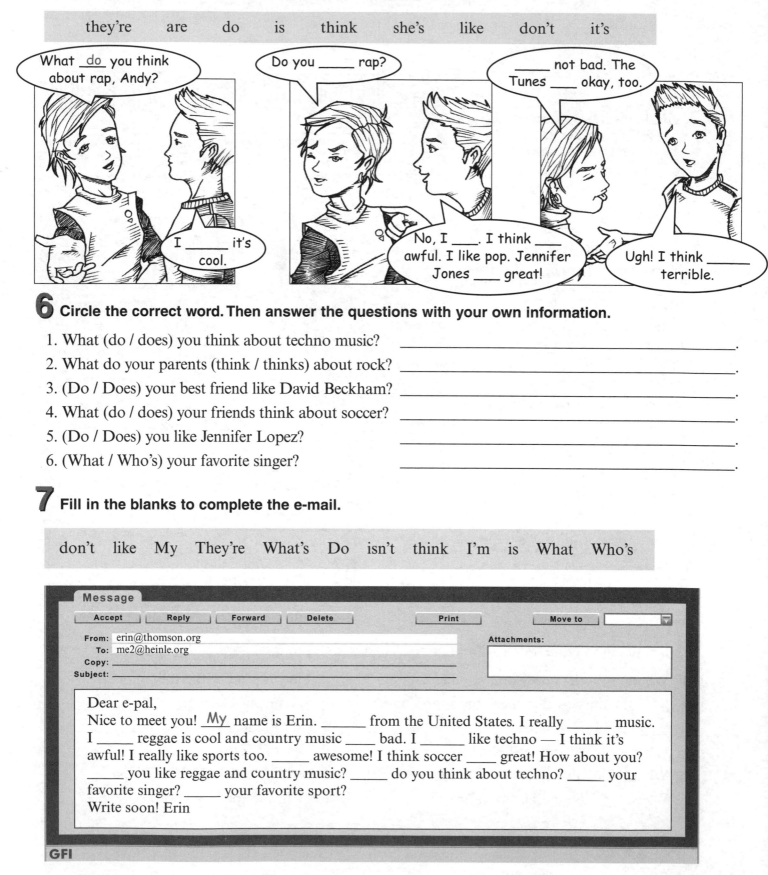

What _do_ you think about rap, Andy?

I _____ it's cool.

Do you _____ rap?

No, I _____. I think _____ awful. I like pop. Jennifer Jones _____ great!

_____ not bad. The Tunes _____ okay, too.

Ugh! I think _____ terrible.

6 Circle the correct word. Then answer the questions with your own information.

1. What (do / does) you think about techno music? _____.
2. What do your parents (think / thinks) about rock? _____.
3. (Do / Does) your best friend like David Beckham? _____.
4. What (do / does) your friends think about soccer? _____.
5. (Do / Does) you like Jennifer Lopez? _____.
6. (What / Who's) your favorite singer? _____.

7 Fill in the blanks to complete the e-mail.

don't   like   My   They're   What's   Do   isn't   think   I'm   is   What   Who's

Message

| Accept | Reply | Forward | Delete | | Print | | Move to | ▼ |

From: erin@thomson.org
To: me2@heinle.org
Copy: _____
Subject: _____

Attachments:

Dear e-pal,
Nice to meet you! _My_ name is Erin. _____ from the United States. I really _____ music.
I _____ reggae is cool and country music ____ bad. I _____ like techno — I think it's
awful! I really like sports too. _____ awesome! I think soccer ____ great! How about you?
_____ you like reggae and country music? _____ do you think about techno? _____ your
favorite singer? _____ your favorite sport?
Write soon! Erin

GFI

Musicians

Read the stories and fill in the boxes below.

Young Crossover Musicians Sell Millions!

Many young classical musicians are *crossing over* (changing) to pop music. Charlotte Church is the world's most successful female classical crossover artist. She was born in Cardiff, Wales, on February 21, 1986. She recorded three classical CDs when she was twelve and thirteen. Her crossover CD, *Voice of an Angel*, came out just after she turned 13. Now she is popular all around the world and has sold over ten million CDs.

Vanessa Mae is another crossover artist. She has sold more than four million CDs. She was born in Singapore in 1978. She began playing the piano when she was three years old. She began playing violin when she was five years old. She also had three classical CDs by age thirteen. Her crossover pop CD came out when she was fourteen. It was called *The Violin Player*.

Name: _____Charlotte Church_____

Born in: _____

Place of birth: _____

Kind(s) of music: _____

Most famous CD: _____

Number of CDs sold: _____

Name: _____

Born in: _____

Place of birth: _____

Kind(s) of music: _____

Most famous CD: _____

Number of CDs sold: _____

Now, give the same information about your favorite musician.

Name: _____

Born in: _____

Place of birth: _____

Kind(s) of music: _____

Most famous CD: _____

Unit 4

What does your father do?

1 **Find 10 professions in the puzzle.**

```
O  H  S  S  I  W  S  I  S  E  S  C  D  S  B  H  C  B
A  B  I  T  E  A  C  H  E  R  D  I  B  S  G  I  A  U
C  P  C  H  W  S  M  S  R  I  P  B  P  T  E  L  I  S
T  M  E  N  A  J  E  R  I  W  Q  U  O  U  T  M  O  I
O  I  I  B  I  I  B  D  L  M  L  O  L  D  S  X  A  N
R  I  C  S  I  B  O  O  H  S  I  I  I  E  M  Z  S  E
B  S  I  S  S  I  C  S  L  K  T  C  N  V  C  Y  S
W  A  I  T  E  R  E  T  I  S  E  W  E  T  L  R  I  S
K  S  F  I  S  W  S  O  C  C  I  O  O  I  P  S  W  M
S  A  L  E  S  P  E  R  S  O  N  F  F  S  U  A  E  A
I  S  R  G  S  I  S  I  I  S  S  E  F  E  D  G  D  N
B  W  L  S  I  G  O  S  G  S  E  I  I  S  Q  J  T  A
B  J  O  U  R  N  A  L  I  S  T  B  C  I  A  K  G  G
B  S  A  W  R  G  R  E  M  M  E  Y  E  I  R  O  A  E
C  O  M  P  U  T  E  R  P  R  O  G  R  A  M  M  E  R
```

2 **Cross out X one word that does not belong in each question and answer. Then match the questions to the answers.**

1. What do does your sisters do? _b_

2. What is does your brother want to be? ___

3. Does Mary want to do be a teacher? ___

4. What's is your job like? ___

5. What do you do want to be? ___

6. Is your mother does a doctor? ___

a. I want to do be a journalist.

b. They're X police officers.

c. Yes, she is not.

d. He is wants to be an actor.

e. It's like interesting.

f. No, she is doesn't.

3 Read about each person. Then (circle) the answer.

1. Maria is a salesperson. She works all day. She doesn't like the job.

   Maria's job is fun. True False

2. Paul is a waiter. He works seven days a week. He is always busy.

   Paul's job is dangerous. True False

3. Gary works for a newspaper. He's a journalist. He likes talking to people. He learns a lot.

   Gary's job is interesting. True False

4. Lee plays in a music group. They play at restaurants. They go to Mexico and Brazil.
   Lee likes his job.

   Lee's job is exciting. True False

5. Alice is a teacher. She has 100 students in her class. She works all day. She reads books
   and prepares classes at night.

   Alice's job is difficult. True False

4 Whose things are these? Read the clues and label the pictures. Then write sentences about each person.

George's father's name is Marco. Marco (M) has one sister and one brother. Marco's brother's name is Frank (F). Marco's sister's name is Helen (H). Helen has one child, Terry (T). George's father is a doctor. Marco's brother wants to be a journalist. Frank's sister is a police officer. George's cousin wants to be a computer programmer.

Marco is a doctor. _____

_____

_____

_____

5 Unscramble the questions and answer them. Use your own information.

1. Q: (do / what / about / think / actors / you) ____What do you think about actors?____
   A: _____
2. Q: (best / a / your / singer / to / does / want / friend / be) _____
   A: _____
3. Q: (parents / do / your / what / do) _____
   A: _____
4. Q: (like / is / what / your / job / favorite) _____
   A: _____

LESSON B A doctor works in a hospital.

6 Draw lines to match the job to the workplace. Then write sentences.

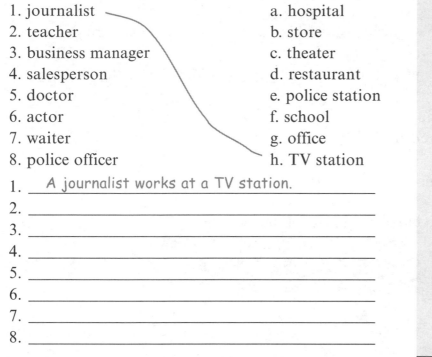

1. journalist
2. teacher
3. business manager
4. salesperson
5. doctor
6. actor
7. waiter
8. police officer

a. hospital
b. store
c. theater
d. restaurant
e. police station
f. school
g. office
h. TV station

1. ___A journalist works at a TV station.___
2. _____
3. _____
4. _____
5. _____
6. _____
7. _____
8. _____

7 Write about these people. Use words from above and the box below.

| stressful | busy | difficult | boring |

Lisa is a waitress. She works in a restaurant. Her job is busy. She wants to be an actor. She wants to work in a theater.

16   JOBS

most	dangerous	least	truck	worker	jobs	pilot	want	driving	construction

The Ten Most Dangerous Jobs

Lots of people __want__ jobs they think are fun or exciting, like being a _____. But flying airplanes is the third most dangerous job in the U.S. An even more _____ job is fishing, and the _____ dangerous job is being a logger — someone who cuts down trees. The number four, six, seven, and nine _____ are all in construction. From the most to the _____ dangerous, the jobs include metal workers, roofers, electricians, and general _____ workers. Another dangerous occupation is at number eight, being a farm _____. Numbers five and ten on the list are _____ jobs. The more dangerous one is being a driver who sells things, like a pizza delivery driver. The less dangerous driving job is being a _____ driver.

Look at the jobs in the box. Which is the most interesting jobs below? Why? Write five sentences.

actor	singer	journalist	pilot	police officer

_____

_____

_____

_____

_____

Review 1

1 Write the missing words in the blanks and in the crossword.

Down

1. A waiter works in a _____.
3.

6. _____ is a kind of music.
8. Shakira is a _pop_ singer.

Across

2.

4. A doctor works in a _____.
5. An _____ works in a theater.
7. She is a police _____.
9.

10. He comes from Thailand. He's _____.

2 Unscramble the sentences. Then number them to make a conversation.

___ of kind is what restaurant it _____

___ no he's not waiter a he's _____

___ works restaurant he a in _____

_1_ Todd is your student a friend?   Is your friend Todd a student?

___ work does where he _____

___ has Italian food it _____

3 Circle the correct word. Then write the question or answer for each. Use your own information if you need to.

1. Q: _____

   A: Her friend (is / isn't) Thai. She's Chinese.

2. Q: _____

   A: My mother (work / works) at a hospital.

3. Q: _____

   A: My friends (like / likes) Mexican food.

4. Q: (Is / Are) your school near a restaurant?

   A: _____

5. Q: (Do / Does) your classmates like classical music?

   A: _____

4 Unscramble the words. Then read the clues and fill in the blanks.

yalti	1. It's between Japan and China. _____
toush roaek	2. It's to the north of Argentina on the map. _____
rabliz	3. It's to the right of Peru on the map. _____
dutine tasset	4. It's between Canada and Mexico. _____
molobaci	5. It's near France. _____

5 Fill in the missing letters to spell a new word. Use the word to fill in the blank and answer the question.

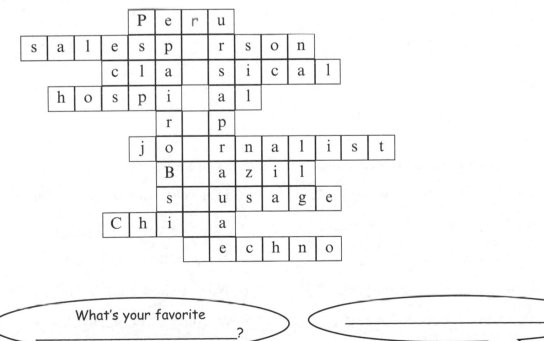

		P	e	r	u				
s	a	l	e	s	p		r	s	o	n
		c	l	a		s	i	c	a	l
	h	o	s	p	i		a	l
				r		p
		j	o		r	n	a	l	i	s	t
				B		a	z	i	l
				s		u	s	a	g	e
	C	h	i		a
				e	c	h	n	o

What's your favorite _____?

_____.

Unit 5

How was your weekend?

1 Draw lines to make verb phrases. Then use the past verb form to make sentences that are true for you.

go   my mother   _____

talk   soccer   _____

watch   my room   _____

do   on the phone   _____

clean   TV   _____

play   my homework   _____

help   shopping   _____Pedro and I went shopping last Tuesday._____

2 Fill in the blanks. Then number the sentences to make a conversation.

___ What _____ you do?

___ On Saturday I _____ TV.

___ Did you _____ anything on Sunday?

___ _____ was the beach?

___ Yes, I did. I _____ to the beach.

_1_ _How_ was your weekend?

___ It _____ okay.

___ The beach _____ great!

3 Circle the correct word. Then match the questions to the answers.

1. What did you (do / did) last weekend? _e_   a. He (went / played) to the beach.

2. Did you (visit / go) your aunt on Sunday? ___   b. Yes, they (do / did).

3. How (was / does) your weekend? ___   c. No, she (didn't / doesn't).

4. (Does / Did) Sara clean her room yesterday? ___ d. No, I visited her (on / at) Friday.

5. What did Darin do (in / on) Saturday? ___   e. We (did / do) homework.

6. Did Mariko and Mika (play / played) soccer? ___ f. It (is / was) busy.

4 **What did Kathy and Dean do last Saturday? Number the pictures in the order they did these activities. Then write sentences.**

Dean practiced piano last Saturday night

_____

_____   _____

5 **Write the questions for the answers below.**

1. Q: ___What did you do last night?_____

   A: I talked on the phone last night.

2. Q: _____

   A: No, I didn't watch TV yesterday. I helped my mom.

3. Q: _____

   A: My friend cleaned her room on Saturday morning.

4. Q: _____

   A: Yes, they did. My classmates always play soccer on Tuesdays.

5. Q: _____

   A: My family went to the beach last weekend.

What did you do yesterday?

6 Fill in the blanks in Marion's diary note. Then complete the chart with her information.

| talked | did | played | went | watched | practiced | helped | visited | go | cleaned | was |

Sunday, August 29th

Wow! Last week __was__ really busy! Last Monday, I _____ piano in the afternoon and _____ my room that night. Then, the next day Lee and I _____ tennis after school. I _____ my cousins in St. Louis four days ago and three days ago my sister and I _____ shopping in the afternoon and _____ three movies that night! The day before yesterday, I _____ my homework all day and yesterday I _____ my mom. This morning I _____ on the phone with my friends in Mexico and Japan! I didn't ___ to the beach this afternoon, I was just too tired!

Marion	
Monday	practiced piano, cleaned her room
Tuesday	
Wednesday	
Thursday	
Friday	
Saturday	
Sunday	

7 What did you do last week? Fill in the chart below. Then write your own diary note.

_____
_____
_____
_____
_____
_____
_____
_____
_____
_____
_____

Me	
Monday	
Tuesday	
Wednesday	
Thursday	
Friday	
Saturday	
Sunday	

Go for it!
Weekend activities

Read the paragraph and answer the questions.

"What did you do last weekend?" Ask thousands of people that question and you get an *average answer* — an idea of what everybody does on the weekend. So, what did the average person do last weekend? Well, 85 percent of the people went to a movie and 68 percent visited an amusement park. Another 51 percent watched a sport of some kind, 35 percent visited a museum and about 15 percent went to a jazz or classical music concert.

But how about everyday chores? Well, the average person worked for about seven and a half hours over the weekend. Some people cleaned, some did laundry, and some cooked (Some even did homework!). People slept for an average of 17 hours last weekend. They also ate and drank for about three hours and watched TV or videos for about four hours a day! This is not good news, especially because the average person only exercised for about 30 minutes last weekend — that's not healthy!

1. What did the most people do last weekend? The least? _____

2. What did 68 percent of the people do last weekend? _____

3. Which was more popular — sports events or museum exhibits? _____

4. What did people do for the longest time? the least amount of time? _____

5. How many hours did the average person watch TV on Saturday? _____

What did you do last weekend?
Fill in the chart about yourself.

Activity	Hours
slept	
ate	
exercised	
watched TV	
studied	
visited friends	

Write about your weekend.

_____

_____

_____

_____

_____

Unit 6

What does your uncle look like?

1 Circle the words in the puzzle. Then use the words to complete the chart below.

short	long hair	straight hair	heavy
young	tall	thin	blue eyes
curly hair	average size	old	

```
S  T  R  A  I  G  H  T  H  A  I  R  M
H  I  S  I  C  F  R  A  I  V  H  T  B
O  A  I  C  U  I  A  E  A  E  D  A  B
R  B  E  A  R  A  L  M  O  R  A  H  R
T  A  I  R  L  O  N  G  H  A  I  R  T
E  A  S  W  Y  I  A  L  I  G  Y  B  A
D  H  A  Y  H  D  I  A  I  E  A  B  L
T  E  A  W  A  I  C  G  I  S  L  I  L
R  A  W  T  I  L  L  E  E  I  O  L  A
R  V  A  H  R  O  U  F  G  Z  N  I  A
C  Y  P  A  A  B  L  U  E  E  Y  E  S
O  C  A  E  P  S  V  W  S  I  B  A  A
L  H  W  V  M  A  R  E  C  A  I  O  A
D  A  A  Y  O  U  N  G  S  R  I  W  B
G  B  Q  M  I  E  A  S  T  H  I  N  J
```

is	has
short	

2 Fill in the blanks with **have, has, is,** or **are.** Then write sentences about people you know that have the same physical characteristic.

1. Derek __has__ curly hair.   _My parents have curly hair._

2. Mary's sisters _____ thin.   _____

3. Their grandfather _____ very old. _____

4. My friend and I _____ brown eyes. _____

5. Tim _____ long hair.   _____

6. Mrs. Jones _____ tall.   _____

3 Unscramble the sentences and number them to make a conversation. Remember to add punctuation.

___ curly really it's

___ long has no doesn't he brown he hair

___ has tall and he brown he's eyes

___ straight it curly is or

___ boyfriend new what look like your does

___ black he have does hair

_____

_____

_____

_____

_____

4 Fill in the blanks. Then match the questions and responses.

1. __Is__ Alex old? __e__

2. What _____ your sisters look like? ___

3. Do your parents ____ blue eyes? ___

4. ____ your brother handsome? ___

5. What ____ your friend Hiro look like? ___

6. ____ your grandparents thin? ___

7. What ____ you look like? ___

8. ____ Kumiko have long hair? ___

a. Yes, he is. He's really cute.

b. I have green eyes and black hair.

c. He's tall. He has brown eyes.

d. No, she doesn't. She has short hair.

e. Yes, he is. He's 96!

f. No, they don't. They have green eyes.

g. They're young and have black hair.

h. No, they're not. They're heavy.

5 What do they look like? Write descriptions for the people below.

Emi   Pedro   Terry   Carla and Kris

_____

_____

_____

_____

LESSON B She's wearing a plaid skirt.

6 Unscramble the clothing words.

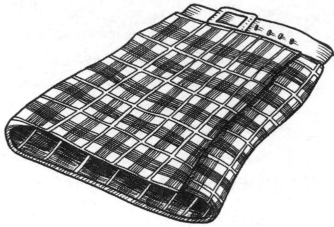

1. stanp _____
2. dialp _____
3. cosks _____
4. ritsk __skirt__
5. sreds _____
6. rispted_____
7. irsht _____
8. kejact_____
9. cedheck_____
10. klpoa tod_____

7 Read about Ted's family and fill in the blanks.

straight	isn't	sister	she's	has	mother	not
wearing	father	he's	he	have	I'm	thin

My _sister_ Louisa is on the left. She's 17 years old. _____very thin and tall. (She's 180
centimeters!) She _____ long, brown, curly hair and blue eyes. She's _____ a shirt, a sweater,
a plaid skirt, and black shoes. My _____ is to the right of Louisa. He's 43 years old. He
_____ very tall, about 160 centimeters. _____ wearing a blue striped jacket, black pants, and
a white shirt. _____ has short, black hair and brown eyes. My _____ is next to my dad. She's
46 years old. She's wearing a polka dot dress and white shoes. She's short and _____. She has
long, _____ hair and big eyes. That's me to the right of my mother. I'm 10 years old and I
_____ straight blonde hair and brown eyes. I'm _____ tall (about 150 centimeters) and
_____ wearing jeans and a T-shirt.

8 Now draw a picture of your family and describe them.

Go for it!
High fashion

Let's go shopping! Look at the catalogue. What items do you like? What items don't you like? Why? Make a list.

S9811
A simple hat is a great way to stay warm and look awesome everywhere! We have hats in checks and men's hats in plaid. All hats only
$9.50

T6934
This cool tie is a great way to show your personality. Especially if you're adventurous!
$1.50

A4287
This cute polka dot shirt is great for spring. Black and white clothes are the style this season!
M3838
This beautiful plaid shirt looks great and keeps you warm. It's a great shirt for winter weather. And, it's inexpensive too. Only
$13.98!

T9878
This checked jacket matches everything! It looks great with a white shirt and black pants. Very nice!
$39.75

I like the . . .	Why?	I don't like the . . .	Why?
polka dot shirt	It's cute.		

Now design three items for the catalogue. Describe them. Remember to add prices!

Unit 7

What's the new student like?

1 Unscramble the adjectives. Then write their opposites in the next column.

	Adjective	Opposite
dkarhwiorgn	hardworking	lazy
edinlfyr		
nufyn		
amne		
toogguin		

2 Fill in the blanks with the words from the box. Then number the sentences to make a conversation.

are	seems	is	doesn't	they're	who	really	she

___ _____ my friends, Shirley and Jean.

___ _____ Jean funny, too?

___ Shy? She _____ seem shy.

___ Well, they're _____ friendly and Shirley's very funny.

___ I know! She _____ outgoing, but she's really shy.

___ What _____ they like?

___ Yes, _____ is. But Jean's a little shy sometimes.

_1_ __Who__ are those girls?

3 Write the questions for the answers below.

1. Q: __Is Erica serious?__

   A: No, she isn't. She seems serious, but she's really shy.

2. Q: _____

   A: No, he isn't mean. Charles is friendly!

3. Q: _____

   A: Peter's shy and Paul's funny.

4. Q: _____

   A: Yes, they're really outgoing.

5. Q: _____

   A: Laura's a little lazy, but she's really nice.

4 Circle the word that does not belong.

1.	nice	lazy	mean	unfriendly
2.	is	has	seems	are
3.	where	like	who	what
4.	outgoing	friendly	funny	shy
5.	hardworking	serious	beautiful	mean
6.	terrible	cool	awesome	great

5 Circle 24 adjectives in Katie's postcard. Then complete the chart about the people she writes about.

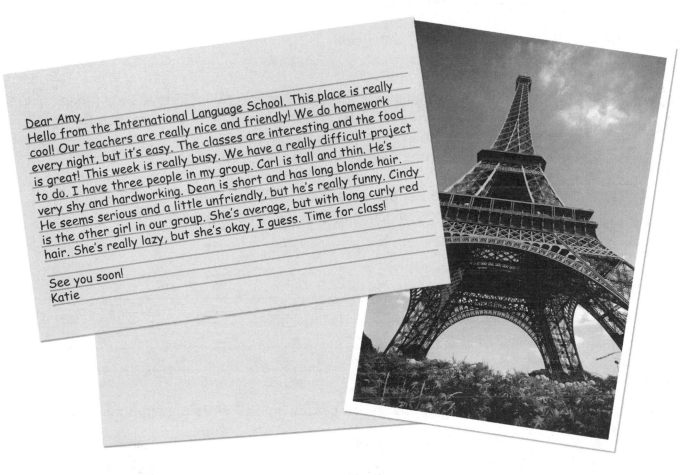

Dear Amy,

Hello from the International Language School. This place is really cool! Our teachers are really nice and friendly! We do homework every night, but it's easy. The classes are interesting and the food is great! This week is really busy. We have a really difficult project to do. I have three people in my group. Carl is tall and thin. He's very shy and hardworking. Dean is short and has long blonde hair. He seems serious and a little unfriendly, but he's really funny. Cindy is the other girl in our group. She's average, but with long curly red hair. She's really lazy, but she's okay, I guess. Time for class!

See you soon!
Katie

Katie's group	Appearance	Personality
Carl		shy and hardworking
Dean		
Cindy		

6 Now describe two people you know.

LESSON B He's really smart.

7 Cross out ✗ one word in each sentence to make it correct. Then write sentences about people you know who have the same personality.

1. My friends Kim and Marta are ~~of~~ kind of shy. _My friend Tina is kind of shy._

2. Ted is not for hardworking at all. He's very lazy! _____

3. Michael is a pretty mean to new students. _____

4. Our teacher is really of outgoing. _____

5. Anna's brother is not very cute. He's really handsome! _____

6. I'm not very athletic at. I hate sports! _____

8 Read the article. Then complete the sentences.

Reading people
You can sometimes understand people by looking at their faces. Do they seem unfriendly? Do they not look at you? Maybe they don't say "hello"—they're probably very shy. Sometimes shy people seem unfriendly. Also, some people can seem mean because they never smile. Maybe they are mean, but maybe they have a serious personality and don't smile a lot. That's okay, too. When people look at you, what do they think?

1. One way you can understand people is by _____.

2. People that seem unfriendly may be _____.

3. Some people seem mean because _____.

4. Someone who seems mean may just be _____.

5. Looking at someone's face can help you _____.

9 Look at these people. What do you think each person is like? Write descriptions below each picture.

He's handsome.
He seems serious.
_____   _____
_____   _____

_____   _____   _____
_____   _____   _____

Characteristics

What other words describe people? Write definitions for the first six words. Then add four words and definitions to the list.

1. energetic _____
2. adventurous _____
3. nervous _____
4. caring _____
5. creative _____
6. unusual _____
7. _____ _____
8. _____ _____
9. _____ _____
10. _____ _____

Write five personality characteristics that are important to you in a friend. List them in order of importance. (1 = most important, 5 = least important)

_____
_____
_____
_____
_____
_____
_____
_____
_____
_____
_____
_____
_____

Now describe your best friend in a paragraph. Why do you like him or her?

_____
_____
_____
_____
_____

Unit 8

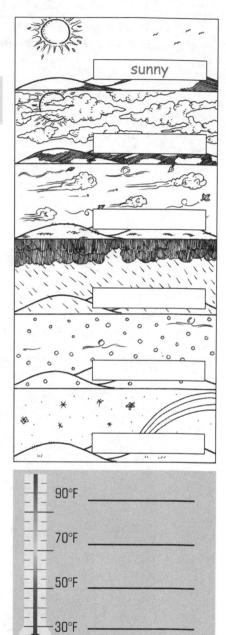

LESSON A
It's cool and sunny here.

1 Circle the words in the puzzle. Then label the pictures with the weather conditions and the thermometer with the temperature words.

cool	sunny	warm	cloudy	windy
rainy	cold	snowy	hot	humid

```
B S S I R S S E S S S I S I
J B I A S U N N Y S S I B C S
I P A C W S M S R I A S I O S
B S I O S I W I N D Y I S L I
T E H O S I S D I S I R S D I
K S F L S W S C A A I S S I L
B W L S I G O L G S E N B S M
B R A I N Y B O I S H O R E E
O H S S I W S U S E O W D S B
S I I B I I B D L M O Y S H R
S I H S I B O Y H S Q I S I S
G B O I W S B E I G L S S S I
I S T G S I S I I W A R M S I
K A H S S H U M I D S R I W B
B W G M S M I E S S B I S S J
```

sunny

90°F _____

70°F _____

50°F _____

30°F _____

2 Draw lines to make verb phrases. Then write sentences about what you or people you know are doing right now.

1. play a   TV
2. talk on the   piano
3. have   sport
4. study   Internet
5. hang out at   phone
6. surf the   lunch
7. practice   home
8. watch   English

I think my brother is playing soccer now.
_____
_____
_____
_____
_____
_____
_____

3 Unscramble these sentences and questions.

1. cold it's rainy studying so I'm and   *It's cold and rainy, so I'm studying.*

2. your are homework doing you _____

3. and what your are brother doing sister _____

4. has always 7:00 breakfast at he _____

5. hot beach so it's we're at the _____

6. I shopping Saturday Shelly go every and _____

4 Read the weather report. Look at the weather conditions on the map and write cold, windy, cloudy, rainy, or hot.

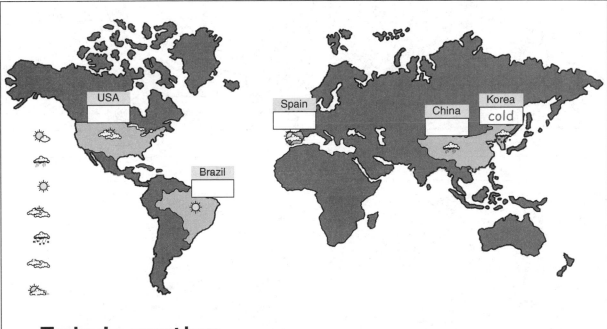

Today's weather

Here is today's weather around the world. It's snowy today in Korea and Japan with temperatures of 23° in Tokyo and an icy 19° in Seoul. In Shanghai, it's raining with a temperature around 39° while Thailand is humid, sunny, and a nice 79°. In most of the United States, the weather today is cloudy with temperatures ranging from 49° in New York to 69° in Los Angeles. Mexico has beautiful, sunny weather today with a temperature of 72°. And down in Brazil and Peru, it's sunny as well, with a temperature of 92° in Sao Paulo and 82° in Cusco. It's windy in Spain today with a temperature of about 50°. And in France it's cloudy and rainy with a temperature of around 45°.

5 Answer these questions with sentences that are true for you.

1. How was the weather last weekend? What did you do? _____

_____

2. How was the weather yesterday? What did you do? _____

_____

3. How's the weather today? What are you doing? _____

_____

LESSON B **What are you doing here?**

6 What season is it? Unscramble the words.

lafl	grinsp	retwin	musmre

1. _____   2. _____   3. _____   4. _____

7 Label the pictures. Then write questions and answers.

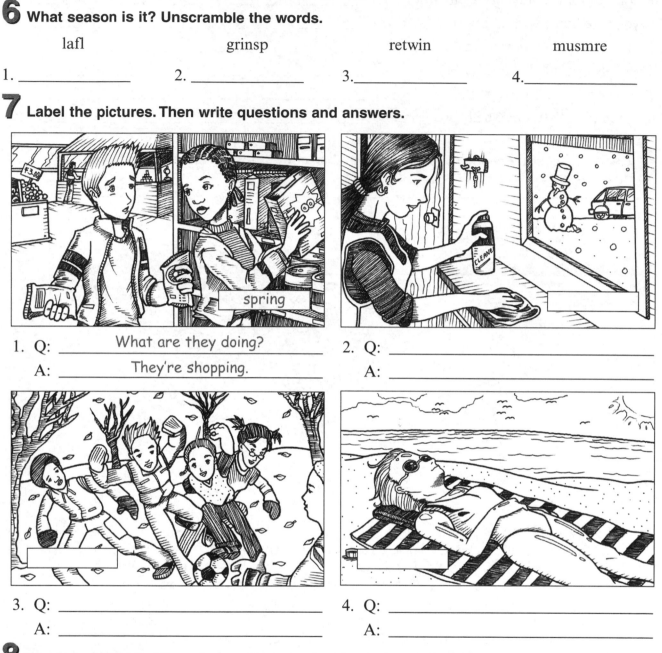

spring

1. Q: _____ What are they doing? _____

   A: _____ They're shopping. _____

2. Q: _____

   A: _____

3. Q: _____

   A: _____

4. Q: _____

   A: _____

8 Read about Maria. Then draw a picture of a friend on holiday. Say what the season is. Then write about what your friend is doing.

It's summer and Maria is having a wonderful vacation in Hawaii. Today she's at the beach. The sun is shining. She is drinking coconut milk.

_____
_____
_____
_____
_____
_____

Go for it!
Weather words

Read about three kinds of clouds.

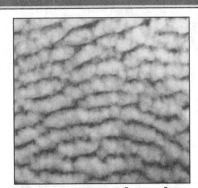

Stratus clouds

are usually low in the sky. We see them when the weather is warm and humid. People often call them rain clouds.

Cirrus clouds

are thin and white. They are usually very high in the sky. We see cirrus clouds when the weather is cool and dry.

Cumulus clouds

are usually very tall and white. Some cumulus clouds are gray in the middle. We often see cumulus clouds on hot summer days. These clouds sometimes turn into rain clouds.

People in the U.S. use Fahrenheit °F for temperatures, not centigrade °C.
Look at the conversion table and complete these equations.

Fahrenheit	Celsius
0	-17.8
10	-12.2
20	-6.7
25	-3.9
32	0
40	4.4
45	7.2
50	10
55	12.8
60	15.6
70	21
80	26.7
85	29.4
90	32.2
95	35
100	37.8
105	40.6
110	43.3

1. $20°\ F\ =\ \_\_°\ C$
2. $\_\_\_°\ F\ =\ 35°\ C$
3. $32°\ F\ =\ \_\_°\ C$
4. $\_°\ F = 10°\ C$
5. $80°\ F = \_\_°\ C$

Fill in a chart about the week's weather where you are.

	Mon.	Tues.	Wed.	Thurs.	Fri.	Sat.	Sun.
Clouds							
Temp ° F							
Temp ° C							
Weather (rainy, windy, etc.)							

Review 2

1 **Write the missing words in the crossword.**

Down

1. My friend Drake is really __funny__.
3. Last Tuesday, the weather was _____.
5. I hate _____ days. I don't like to stay inside.
8. He's not thin, he's _____.
9. It's 19° today. It's _____.
11. It's _____ in Australia in December
12. Yesterday, I _____ my teacher clean up.

Across

2. Are you wearing _____ with those shoes?
4. Kerry's _____ . I don't like her at all!
6. My grandfather is 96. He's pretty _____.
7. My cousin isn't outgoing. He's really _____.
10. My favorite season is winter. I love _____ weather.
13. The waiters here are really _____. It's my favorite restaurant.
14. It's 3:00 in the morning, so I'm _____!

(Crossword grid with answer: 1 Down = f/u/n/n/y)

2 **Unscramble the sentences and rewrite them as questions and answers. Remember to add punctuation!**

1. go on Mary shopping did Saturday — Q: _Did Mary go shopping on Saturday?_
2. wearing a black he's jacket white and — A: _____
3. watched on a movie I Saturday — Q: _____
4. the was so it went park to she sunny — A: _____
5. you what did weekend do last — Q: _____
6. wearing Alberto is what today — A: _____

3 Match the phrases to make sentences.

1. It's beautiful today, so we're having ___
2. My friend Emi has ___
3. Is that journalist mean and ___
4. We went to the beach on ___
5. It's cold this afternoon, so I'm ___
6. Did you talk to your aunt ___
7. It's Sunday night, so Mary's doing ___
8. Jennifer is really tall and ___

a. Saturday.
b. on the phone?
c. wearing a sweater.
d. her homework.
e. long, straight hair.
f. thin.
g. lunch outside.
h. unfriendly?

4 What's wrong with these pictures? Write your answers.

_____
_____
_____
_____

_____
_____
_____
_____

5 Fill in the missing letters to spell a new word. Then write sentences with the words.

				f	u	n	n	y
s	w	e	a	t	e			
				n		c	e	
a	v	e	r	a	g			
				s	u		n	y
p	l	a	y	e				
			t	a		k	e	d
			e		e	s		

MaryAnne is really funny.
_____
_____
_____
_____
_____
_____

6 Change or cross out one word in each phrase to make it correct. Then number the phrases to make a conversation.

___ Very funny! When's Melissa doing tonight? _____

___ He's not really nice, and smart too. _____

___ I'm talking at the phone to you! _____

___ What's he? _____

___ He's the cute new exchange student from French! _____

___ I think she's watched a movie with Kevin. _____

___ Wow! What's he look? _____

_1_ Hello, Karen. ~~What's~~ are you doing? __What__

___ Gee, I'd likes to meet him! _____

My reading journal 1

Circle the correct word or phrase in each group.

Big Cat Adventure is a story by (Charles Dickens / Jeremy Taylor / Jane Austen).

It is a story about two children playing (football / the piano / with a toy car) near

some boats. There are two nice adults in the story. They know a lot about (pumas

/ bicycles / football). There are two pumas in the story — their names are

(Ronaldo / Koko / David) and (Teo / Leo / Feo). There are also some bad people in

the story. Their boss always (studies English / plays the piano / eats candy).

Make sentences about the people in the story.

Professor Gatti

The boss

Yoshi

Tessie

Yoshi has a friend named Tessie.

FACT FILE! Add the Information.

My favorite person in the story is: _____

Name:

Nationality:

Likes…

Hates…

Favorite animals:

What does he / she look like?

What does his / her personality seem like?

Self-check 1

1 Now I can say . . .
Write the questions for these answers.

1. _____
2. _____
3. _____
4. _____
5. _____

a. I'm Japanese.
b. Yes. I'd like onions but not mushrooms.
c. I went to a concert last night.
d. My brother is really smart and very tall.
e. He's visiting his cousin.

2 Now I can talk about . . .
Check the boxes and write an example.

☐ prices _____
☐ directions _____
☐ jobs _____
☐ recent past events _____
☐ what people are doing _____

3 Now I can list . . .
Fill in the chart with words about each topic.

Nationalities	Food	Music	Jobs	Weather
_____	_____	_____	_____	_____
_____	_____	_____	_____	_____
_____	_____	_____	_____	_____
_____	_____	_____	_____	_____
_____	_____	_____	_____	_____

4 Now I can describe . . .
Write words that you know that describe appearance and personality.

Appearance

Personality

Unit 9 LESSON A
Where did you go on vacation?

1 Complete these sentences.

1. He went to summer   a. home.
2. I visited   b. camp.
3. She went to the   c. my uncle.
4. We stayed   d. mountains.
5. They went to   e. New York City.

2 Fill in the blanks with these words.

to	play	go	your	the	do

1. A: Did you _go_ to the movies?

   B: Yes, I did.

2. A: Did you visit _____ uncle?

   B: No, I didn't.

3. A: Did you _____ volleyball?

   B: Yes, I did.

4. A: Did you go to _____ movies?

   B: No, we didn't.

5. A: Did you _____ your homework?

   B: Yes, we did.

6. A: Did you go _____ New York City?

   B: No, we didn't.

3 Fill in the blanks to complete the conversations.

A: Where _did_ you go on vacation?

B: We _____ to London, England.

A: What did you _____ there?

B: We _____ some great exhibits and _____ a lot of photos.

A: Did you _____ anything?

B: Yes, we _____. We _____ some reggae CDs.

A: Did you _____ up early every day?

B: No, we _____. We _____ up late the last day there.

4 **Use the cues to write sentences about yourself or people you know.**

1. (get up early / yesterday)   My father got up early yesterday.

2. (swim / last summer) _____

3. (buy a new sweater / last fall) _____

4. (see a museum exhibit / last year) _____

5. (write some e-mails / this week) _____

6. (read a magazine / last weekend) _____

7. (eat fruit for breakfast / today) _____

8. (take some photos / this month) _____

5 **Circle the correct word in each sentence. Then number the sentences to make a conversation.**

___ (What / Where) did you go?

___ Did you (write / wrote) a postcard to me?

___ Oh, we (go / went) shopping a lot.

_1_ Hi, John. (Do / (Did)) you have a good vacation?

___ So (what / where) did you do there?

___ What did you (buy / bought)?

___ Yes, I (do / did). It was great.

___ I bought (some / any) books and postcards.

___ We (go / went) to the city.

___ No, I didn't write (some / any) postcards - I only bought them!

6 **Read about Andrew's vacation. Fill in the blanks with the correct form of the verb in parentheses. Then answer the questions.**

> Dear Marcie,
> Hello from Hawaii! The weather here is really warm and sunny! We are visiting my dad's friend now, but we _went_ (go) to the mountains to camp last week. Yesterday I _____ (get up) early, _____ (play) tennis with my mom and then _____ (swim) in the afternoon.
>
> Today I _____ (eat) dinner at the beach café and _____ (write) some postcards to my friends. I _____ (have) dinner at Rick's Café, the same restaurant where we went yesterday. The food _____ (be) delicious! I sleep late every day. Why? It's vacation!
> Andrew

1. Where did Andrew go on vacation? _____

2. How was the weather? _____

3. Where did Andrew go his first week there? _____

4. What did he do the day before he wrote the postcard? _____

5. Where did he have lunch? _____

Lesson B How was New York?

7 **Circle the correct word. Then unscramble the words to fill in the blanks.**

| tiuebaflu | epach | lynrfide | venepisex | nealc | elisicudo | drocwed |

1. The pictures at the museum (was /(were)) __beautiful__ .

2. We ate a lot. The food (was / were) _____ .

3. The people at the beach (was / were) very _____ .

4. We didn't shop much. The stores (was / were) very _____ .

5. The park (was / were) _____ for the concert.

6. We bought some T-shirts. They (was / were) _____ .

7. The hotel (was / were) really _____ . The rooms (was / were) really _____ too.

8 **Where did these people go? What did they do? How was it? Use the words in the box to write about them.**

| crowded | mountains | beach | play volleyball | beautiful |
| cheap | city | rain | go camping | restaurant |

_____   _____   _____
_____   _____   _____
_____   _____   _____

9 **Write about your last vacation. Where did you go? What did you do? How was it?**

_____
_____
_____
_____
_____

Go for it!
Travel trends

Read the article and fill in the information below.

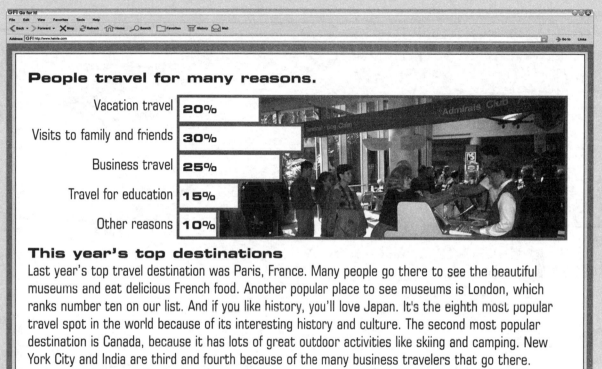

People travel for many reasons.

Vacation travel	**20%**
Visits to family and friends	**30%**
Business travel	**25%**
Travel for education	**15%**
Other reasons	**10%**

This year's top destinations

Last year's top travel destination was Paris, France. Many people go there to see the beautiful museums and eat delicious French food. Another popular place to see museums is London, which ranks number ten on our list. And if you like history, you'll love Japan. It's the eighth most popular travel spot in the world because of its interesting history and culture. The second most popular destination is Canada, because it has lots of great outdoor activities like skiing and camping. New York City and India are third and fourth because of the many business travelers that go there. And Las Vegas, Australia, and Hawaii, are numbers five, six, and seven because of the exciting and interesting things to see, and do there. The second to last place on our list, Cuba, is popular simply for its beautiful scenery and friendly people. The music is great, too!

Why do you travel? _____

The top 10 destinations

1. _____   6. _____
2. _____   7. _____
3. _____   8. _____
4. _____   9. _____
5. _____   10. _____

The top 5 cities I'd like to visit   Why?

1. _____   _____
2. _____   _____
3. _____   _____
4. _____   _____
5. _____   _____

Unit 10 LESSON A
I love this scarf!

1 **Find these and other gift ideas in the puzzle. Circle the words.**

```
K A H E A D P H O N E S I S W
G C F I W A B E I G L A P U I
I A R G U I T A R I I A O N C
B M L A I G S A G A E G S G M
B E H I S I C R I S H A T L E
O R S A B R A C E L E T E A A
A A I B I I R A L M O A R S R
A I C A I B F B H A Q I S S A
B A I A S I T C D P L A Y E R
Z E E A R R I N G S C A I S D
B A A I R N E C K L A C E A A
J B I C A A P S V A S I B A A
```

camera

guitar   sunglasses   posters

bracelet   headphones   CD player

2 **Check ✓ the sentences that are correct. Put an ✗ next to the sentences that are not correct and rewrite them.**

1. I likes her old earrings. ✗ <u>I like her old earrings.</u>

2. Mary loves your new checked scarf. ____ _____

3. His friends can't like the green guitar. ____ _____

4. We can't stand her purple necklace, too. ____ _____

5. Henry don't mind her big sunglasses. ____ _____

6. Do you like that headphones? ____ _____

7. Does your sister like this camera? ____ _____

3 **Fill in the blanks in the conversations.**

1. A: __Do__ you like Anna's scarf?
   B: No, I don't like ___ at all.

2. A: _____ Ken and Ali like Keanu Reeves?
   B: Yes, they love _____!

3. A: I _____ stand her sunglasses.
   B: I don't like them, _____.

4. A: Rita really _____ rock.
   B: I like it, _____.

5. A: _____ Nancy like movies?
   B: Yes, she loves _____.

6. A: ____ you like Monica Seles?
   B: Yes, I like _____ a lot.

4 Read Ian's e-mail and circle the things he likes. Then write True or False and rewrite the false answers to make them correct.

```
┌─────────────────────────────────────────────────────────────────────────────────┐
│  Message                                                                          │
│  ┌────────┐ ┌────────┐ ┌──────────┐ ┌────────┐      ┌────────┐    ┌──────────┐ ┌──▼─┐
│  │ Accept │ │ Reply  │ │ Forward  │ │ Delete │      │  Print │    │ Move to  │ │    │
│  └────────┘ └────────┘ └──────────┘ └────────┘      └────────┘    └──────────┘ └────┘
│     From: _____   Attachments:                 │
│       To: _____  ┌──────────────────────────┐  │
│     Copy: _____  │                          │  │
│  Subject: _____  │                          │  │
│                                                      └──────────────────────────┘  │
│  ┌──────────────────────────────────────────────────────────────────────────────┐ │
│  │  Dear Alisha,                                                                  │ │
│  │  Guess what? I got $100 for my birthday! I want to buy something — but what? What do │
│  │  you think about that new Pro-One camera we saw last weekend? I love it! I take a lot of │
│  │  pictures and my old camera is terrible! But it's $175 — that's pretty expensive! I don't │
│  │  mind that new Grange guitar. It's pretty cool, but I can't stand the color. It's pink! The │
│  │  new Sono CD player we saw at More Music is great, too. I don't like most new CD players │
│  │  because they're too big. I don't mind the Sono because it's really cool and small, and the │
│  │  headphones are awesome! I don't know what to buy! What do you think?          │ │
│  │  Call me later!                                                                │ │
│  │  Ian                                                                           │ │
│  │                                                                                │ │
│  └──────────────────────────────────────────────────────────────────────────────┘ │
│  GFI                                                                               │
└─────────────────────────────────────────────────────────────────────────────────┘
```

1. _False_ Ian doesn't like taking pictures.   _Ian likes taking pictures._

2. _____ The Pro-One camera is cheap. _____

3. _____ Ian likes the guitar. _____

4. _____ He likes the color of the guitar. _____

5. _____ Ian thinks most CD players are awesome. _____

6. _____ Ian likes the headphones a lot. _____

5 Look at the chart below. Fill in number 5 about yourself. Then write a sentence about what each person thinks of these things.

☺ = likes   😐 = doesn't mind   ☹ = can't stand

Name	Music		Food		Activities	
1. Michael	rap	☺	sandwiches	☺	camping	☹
2. Jane	classical	☹	salads	☹	swimming	😐
3. Tony	salsa	😐	french fries	☺	taking pictures	☹
4. Jessica	rock	☹	spaghetti	😐	surfing the Net	☺
5.						

1. _Michael likes rap and he likes sandwiches, but he can't stand camping._

2. _____

3. _____

4. _____

5. _____

LESSON B What would you like for your birthday?

6 Unscramble the words. Then complete the chart.

nisetn teckar   celetrocin zoriganre   dracalen   zlupze

puticer meraf   loccohtesa   welfors

Gifts I'd like	Why?	Gifts I wouldn't like	Why?

7 Order the sentences to make a conversation.

No, I wouldn't. They're boring.

I'd like that electronic organizer, but it's expensive.

That sounds fun. I love it!

I like it, too.

I don't like them either. How about that puzzle?

What would you like for your birthday?

Yes, it's not cheap. Would you like those headphones?

A: <u>What would you like for your birthday?</u>

B: _____

A: _____

B: _____

A: _____

B: _____

A: _____

8 Make a Birthday Wish List for five people you know. Then write sentences.

Name	Would like	Why?
Mary	tennis racket	She loves sports.

1. _____ My sister Mary would like a tennis racket because she loves sports.

2. _____

3. _____

4. _____

5. _____

Go for it!
Gift giving

Look at the gift ideas. Then write the items in the section you think is most appropriate. Some items may be used more than once.

movie posters   handmade bracelets   music   jewelry
puzzles   CDs and videos   flowers   chocolates
electronic items   socks   winter jacket sports tickets

GFI Go for it!
File   Edit   View   Favorites   Tools   Help
Back ▾ Forward ▾ Stop Refresh Home Search Favorites History Mail
Address GFI http://www.heinle.com   Go to Links

Gift Ideas for Teens

Teenagers are great, but buying the right present is difficult sometimes! With these awesome gift ideas, it's easy!

Gift Ideas for Mom

Mom helps us so much and we want to give her a great gift! Here are some interesting and thoughtful gift ideas for Mom!

Gift Ideas for Dad

Surprise the man in your life with these great gift ideas for dads of all ages!

Name	Personality / Looks	Gift idea
Rico	outgoing, friendly, handsome	
Patty	shy, quiet, loves movies	
Judy	smart, hardworking, loves computers	

Add two of your friends to the list and describe them. What gifts do you think are best for everyone on the list?

Unit 11 LESSON A
Can I bring my cell phone to school?

1 **Fill in the letters to make words. Match the words to make verb phrases.**

r _u_ n   _ _ o u r c e l _ p _ one   _____run in the hallway_____

w _ _ a r   j e _ n _   _____

_ r r i _ e   _ o m u _ i _   _____

_ i s _ e n   a _ e s _   _____

e a _   _i n t h _e_ h a _l_ l w a y   _____

_ r i _ g   l a _ _   _____

_ a k _   i _ c _ a s _   _____

2 **Fill in the blanks with can or can't. Then number the sentences to make a conversation.**

___ No phones? _____ we leave our cell phones in our bags?

___ Okay. _____ we talk on our cell phones after class, too?

_1_ Mr. Smith, _____ we listen to music in class?

___ Yes, you _____ . But you _____ bring them to class.

___ No, you _____. You _____ listen to it after class.

___ Yes, you _____ . But you _____ bring bags to class.

3 **Write the questions.**

1. Q: _____

    A: No, you can't. You can talk on it before or after class.

2. Q: _____

    A: Yes, we can bring our lunch. But we can't eat in class.

3. Q: _____

    A: No, they can't wear jeans at my cousin's school.

4. Q: _____

    A: Yes, you can run outside, but you can't run in the hallways.

5. Q: _____

    A: No, my sister can't arrive late for class.

4 Use the cues to make a list of school rules. Circle the rules you have at your school.

SCHOOL RULES

1. (no / jeans) _____Don't wear jeans._____

2. (no / fight) _____

3. (wear / uniforms) _____

4. (no / mess) _____

5. (clean up / after class) _____

6. (eat / in lunchroom) _____

7. (no / run in the hallway) _____

8. (be quiet / in class) _____

5 Look at the list of rules above. What rules are the students in this picture breaking?

1. _____Takuya is listening to music. He can't listen to music in class. He has to be quiet._____

2. _____

3. _____

4. _____

5. _____

6 Read about this unusual school and fill in the blanks. Then compare five things about Peter's school with your school.

| eats | listens | has | doesn't | goes | loves | can | studies | plays | can't | do | get |

Peter _____ to an interesting school. He _____ at home and his mother is his teacher! He _____ have to wear a uniform, he _____ wear jeans and a T-shirt to school. He has class in his living room and he _____ soccer with his brother for PE. Peter _____ music, so he _____ to music in class every day. At noon, Peter _____ lunch in the living room. But home school isn't always easy. Peter _____ to study hard and he has to _____ his homework, too. School starts early at 7:00 a.m. Peter _____ arrive late, so he has to _____ up at 6:00 a.m. every day.

1. (wear) _____Peter doesn't have to wear a uniform. I don't have to wear a uniform, either._____

2. (music) _____

3. (play soccer for PE) _____

4. (eat lunch) _____

5. (do homework) _____

6. (late) _____

7. (get up early) _____

LESSON B I have to clean the living room.

7 Read about Angela's rules. Fill in the blanks. Then write down Angela's rules.

Message						
Accept	Reply	Forward	Delete	Print	Move to	▼

From: _____
To: _____
Copy: _____
Subject: _____

Attachments:

Dear Molly,

My parents don't let me do anything, either. I can't _go_ to a movie alone and I can't
_____ TV on school nights. I have to _____ my homework every day after school. At night,
I have to _____ the piano, and I have to _____ the dishes after dinner. I can _____ the Net
for fun, but I have to _____ to bed before 9:30. I have to _____ my room every day, too. I
guess it's okay. My family is cool, and I can _____ out with friends on the weekends, but I
have to _____ home by 6:00 p.m. That's okay, my family and I have lots of fun at home.

Angela, 13, Brighton England

GFI

1. _Don't go to the movies alone._____
2. _____
3. _____
4. _____
5. _____
6. _____
7. _____
8. _____

8 Make a list of five rules you have at home.

_____
_____
_____
_____
_____

Signs

Look at these signs and write a rule for each one. Then write where you would find these signs.

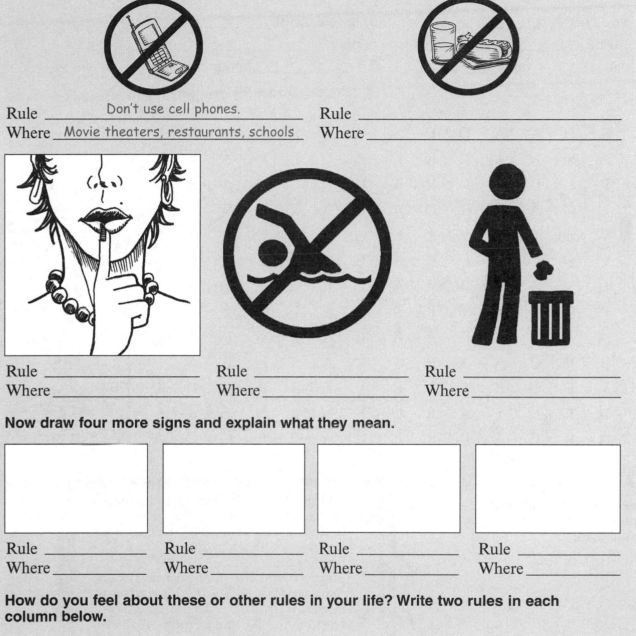

Rule _____ Don't use cell phones. _____   Rule _____
Where _ Movie theaters, restaurants, schools _   Where _____

Rule _____   Rule _____   Rule _____
Where _____   Where _____   Where _____

Now draw four more signs and explain what they mean.

Rule _____   Rule _____   Rule _____   Rule _____
Where _____   Where _____   Where _____   Where _____

How do you feel about these or other rules in your life? Write two rules in each column below.

Like	Don't mind	Can't stand

Unit 12

How often do you exercise?

1 Find the missing words to fill in the blanks in the phrases below. Circle the missing words in the puzzle.

1. go _running_
2. take a _____ and _____
3. eat _____ and _____
4. get _____

5. have a healthy _____
6. play _____
7. _____ on junk food
8. _____ up late

```
Z  E  H  C  A  D  E  N  W  I  S  S  A  B  I
K  A  S  N  A  C  K  I  C  C  I  L  A  I  L
A  I  I  B  I  I  B  A  L  M  C  A  A  H  R
A  I  C  A  I  B  O  R  H  A  K  I  S  I  A
B  W  S  T  A  Y  E  E  G  A  E  G  B  A  M
B  C  H  I  S  I  B  L  I  B  R  E  A  K  A
O  H  S  A  I  W  A  A  J  E  A  C  D  A  F
S  P  O  R  T  S  I  X  U  L  I  S  Y  B  R
B  A  A  B  R  E  A  K  F  A  S  T  I  A  U
J  B  I  C  A  A  P  S  K  A  S  I  B  A  I
I  V  E  G  E  T  A  B  L  E  S  P  C  H  T
G  B  F  I  T  A (R  U  N  N  I  N  G) B  S
I  A  R  G  A  I  S  I  I  A  A  I  C  E  A
```

2 Look at Marta's planner and compare her schedule with your own.

> Monday, Wednesday, Friday, and Saturday from 4:00 - 5:30, *play soccer*
> Every day from 7:00 - 8:00, *do homework*
> Tuesday and Thursday from 5:00 - 6:00, *practice piano*
> Sunday from 1:00 - 3:00, *help mom*
> Saturday from 10:00 - 11:00, *clean room*
> Monday from 6:30 - 7:30 and Saturday from 1:00 - 2:00, *study English*

1. _Marta helps her mom once a week. I help my mom once a week, too._____
2. _____
3. _____
4. _____
5. _____
6. _____

3 Mark the correct place for the adverb or expression in each answer. Then write the questions.

1. Q: _How often does Mary usually exercise?_
   A: (usually) Mary ✗ exercises three times a week.

2. Q: _____
   A: (twice a year) I go to the dentist.

3. Q: _____
   A: (never) No, he doesn't. Michael takes a break.

4. Q: _____
   A: (always) No, my friends hate junk food. They eat healthy food.

5. Q: _____
   A: (four times a week) The volleyball team plays in the summer.

4 Circle the correct word. Number the sentences to make a conversation.

_____ We usually (watch / watches) *Manta*.

_1_ Manolo, do you (take / ever) stay up late?

_____ I usually read, or my brother and I watch TV once in a (time / while).

_____ Yes, I do. I stay up late at (every / least) four nights a week.

_____ Wow, that's pretty often. What do you usually (do / does)?

_____ What (do / does) you usually watch?

_____ *Manta?* I watch that (all / three) the time!

5 Read about John. Circle the things he does. Underline the things he doesn't do. Then write True or False for each statement and correct the false sentences.

Some of my friends play sports seven days a week, but I hardly ever play sports. I never work out, either. I can't stand exercise! I play volleyball at the beach once a week. It's my favorite sport. I go swimming two or three times a month, but I never go running — I hate it! I like to relax. I listen to music all the time. I sometimes feel tired after school, so I usually take a break and watch TV. But I have to study every day — it's a rule at my house!

1. _False_ John plays sports seven days a week. _John hardly ever plays sports._

2. _____ He plays volleyball once a month. _____

3. _____ He always goes swimming. _____

4. _____ He listens to music all the time. _____

5. _____ He usually takes a break after school. _____

6. _____ He has to study every day. _____

LESSON B What do you do for fun?

6 Fill in the blanks with the correct verb. Then write sentences about you or people you know.

1. _____ volleyball _My cousin plays volleyball four times a week in summer._____

2. _____ swimming _____

3. _____ board games _____

4. _____ aerobics _____

5. _____ roller blading _____

6. _____ karate _____

7 Read the cartoon and fill in the blanks. Then complete the chart.

Alan: So, Brenda, what do you _____ for fun?

Brenda: Oh, I sometimes _____ basketball and I _____ skateboarding once in a while. How about you, Alan?

Alan: Well, I hardly ever _____ skateboarding, but I _____ karate sometimes. And I _____ soccer all the time.

Brenda: Me too! I love soccer. I _____ aerobics all the time, too.

Alan: I don't like working out, but I _____ running once in a while.

Brenda: I hardly ever _____ running. I'm too busy!

	all the time	sometimes	hardly ever	once in a while
Brenda				
Alan				
Me				

8 Now add your own information to the chart above and write about what you do for fun.

_____

_____

_____

Go for it!
Food pyramid

Look at the food pyramid. Add two foods to each food group.

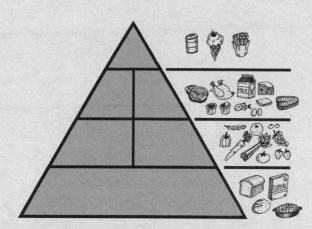

Sugars: _____

_____

Dairy and protein: _____

_____

_____

Fruits and vegetables: _____

_____

_____

Starches (bread, cereal, pasta): ___

_____

How often do you eat these foods?

Sugars: _____ I hardly ever eat sugar. _____

Dairy and protein: _____

Fruits and vegetables: _____

Starches (bread, cereal, pasta): _____

What's your favorite meal? Write a description then fill in the blanks. Then count how many servings of each food group it has.

My favorite meal: _____

- Sugars = ___ servings.
- Dairy = ___ servings.
- Meat = ___ servings.

- Vegetables = ___ servings.
- Fruit = ___ servings.
- Bread, cereal, rice, pasta = ___ servings.

What do you eat in one week? Keep a food diary. Then write about your eating habits.

	Mon	Tues	Wed	Thurs	Fri	Sat	Sun
Breakfast							
Lunch							
Dinner							
Snacks							

On Monday I had yogurt and an apple for breakfast, a sandwich for lunch and a
steak and salad for dinner. I didn't have any snacks. It was a pretty healthy day.
On Tuesday...

Review 3

1 Complete the crossword.

Across

1. She wears a _____ and a watch on her arm.
5. I saw some great museum _____ in Italy.
8. The paintings at the art _____ were beautiful.
9. Let's go to the mountains and go _____.
11. She has a black and white _____ around her neck.
13. I get up _____ every day.

Down

2. He's not early, he's _____.
3. I don't want to swim today. I _____ yesterday.
4. Eat lots of fruit and _____. It's really healthy!
6. Take a _____ and relax sometimes.
7. _____ food is not healthy.
10. I have a great music _____ on my wall.
11. I usually _____ on fruit between lunch and dinner.
12. When I'm tired, I _____ and watch TV.

2 Unscramble the sentences. Then write about yourself.

1. (every Tuesday I usually swim) _I usually swim every Tuesday._____
   Me: _I do, too._____

2. (wear we to always English headphones in class have) _____
   Me: _____

3. (the in often I snack afternoon) _____
   Me: _____

4. (in I running go the once a while in park) _____
   Me: _____

5. (lot I a chocolate like) _____
   Me: _____

3 Fill in the blanks. Then number the sentences to make a conversation.

___ Do you _____ to wear a uniform at your school?
___ No, we don't. We _____ wear jeans at my school.
_1_ Hi, Janice. What are you _____?
___ Hello, Cindy. _____ shopping for new school clothes.
___ No jeans? Can you _____ bracelets and earrings?
___ Yes, we can wear bracelets, _____ we can't wear earrings.
___ Really? We _____ wear jeans at all!

4 What did these people do last weekend? Look at the pictures and write two sentences about each. Use the words in the box.

| go camping | relax | read a book | shopping | buy a sweater | play guitar |

_____   _____   _____

_____   _____   _____

_____   _____   _____

5 Fill in the missing letters to spell a new word.

		c	a	m	e	r	a	s	
	s		o	p	p	i	n	g	
j	u	n	k	f		o	d		
				a	m	p	i	n	g
	u	n	i	f		r	m	s	
			f		o	w	e	r	s
b	o	a	r	d	g		m	e	s
		g	u	i		a	r	s	
		m	u	s		u	m	s	

6 Now write sentences with seven words from 5. Use love, like, don't mind, or can't stand.

1. _I like cameras. I take a lot of pictures._

2. _____

3. _____

4. _____

5. _____

6. _____

7. _____

Unit 13

LESSON A
I have a headache.

1 Label the parts of the body. Then complete the chart below.

I have a sore _____.	I have a _____ache.

2 Fill in the blanks. Use the words in the box.

see a dentist   eat anything   go to bed early   drink tea with honey   lie down and rest

1. A: She has a headache.

   B: She should ___lie down and rest.___

2. A: I have a stomachache.

   B: You shouldn't _____.

3. A: He has a toothache.

   B: He should _____.

4. A: She has a sore throat.

   B: She should _____.

5. A: I'm tired.

   B: You should _____.

3 Change one word in each answer to make it correct. Then write the questions.

1. Q: _____Do you have a headache?_____

   A. No, I doesn't have a headache. I have a cough. ___don't___

2. Q: _____

   A. Yes, he should stays home. _____

3. Q: _____

   A: No, Alex doesn't have a sore arm. He has an sore head. _____

4. Q: _____

   A: George has a hurt throat. _____

5. Q: _____

   A: No, we should go home. We should go to the hospital. _____

4 Number the monsters.

The first monster has a long neck and three eyes. It has one big ear and three big teeth. The second monster has a small head and big hands and feet. It has a big eye on each hand. The third monster has a big nose and one eye. It has four arms and only one leg. The fourth monster has two hands on each arm and a big stomach.

5 Read the conversation. Write T for True or F for False. Then correct the false sentences.

John: Hey, Perry. How are you?

Perry: Not too good. I have sore feet.

John: Why are your feet sore?

Perry: I went camping last weekend.

John: Did you go to the mountains?

Perry: Yes. My back is sore, too.

John: You should take it easy.

Perry: I know, but I have to play basketball.

John: Don't go! You should stay home tonight.

1. ____ Perry has sore feet and a sore arm.

   _____

2. ____ John went camping last weekend.

   _____

3. ____ Perry went to the mountains.

   _____

4. ____ Perry has to play basketball.

   _____

5. ____ Perry thinks John should see a doctor tonight.

   _____

LESSON B **You should relax.**

6 Complete the conversation under each picture.

1

A: What's the matter with __her__ ?
B: She's really _____.
A: She should _____.

2

A: What's wrong with _____?
B: He's pretty _____.
A: He shouldn't _____.

3

A: What's the matter with _____?
B: They're really _____.
A: They should _____.

4

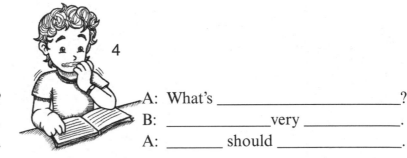

A: What's _____?
B: _____ very _____.
A: _____ should _____.

5

A: _____
B: _____
A: _____

6

A: _____
_____
B: _____
_____
A: _____
_____

7 Unscramble these sentences.

1. nervous I'm I test because a have tomorrow. __I'm nervous because I have a test tomorrow.__

2. difficult is my because is friend homework her confused. _____

3. sad we're we tonight out can't go because. _____

4. can't play games bored video because he's he. _____

5. stressed she's is busy because her job really. _____

8 How are you today? Why do you feel that way?

_____
_____
_____
_____
_____

Go for it!
Doctors

Read about a trip to the doctor and fill in the table.

A good visit to the doctor

Many people get stressed out or confused at the doctor's office, but they don't want to ask too many silly questions. Asking questions is okay. You should go to a doctor who doesn't make you nervous. Also, before you go to the doctor, write a list of your problems and questions. This makes it easier to remember everything you want to know.

Sometimes a doctor will give you medicine. He or she should explain what the medicine does and be sure it's safe for you. Your doctor may send you to a special doctor for more medical tests. There are many kinds of special doctors, and each one should explain what the tests are for and how they will be done..

A good doctor…

_____
_____
_____
_____
_____

There are many kinds of doctors. Match the names with their specialties.

1. dermatologist
2. ophthalmologist
3. podiatrist
4. pediatrician
5. cardiologist

a. eye doctor
b. heart doctor
c. children's doctor
d. skin doctor
e. foot doctor

Do you like going to the doctor? Why or why not?

_____
_____
_____
_____
_____

What are you doing this summer?

1 **Find these words in the puzzle. Then fill in the blanks below.**

camping	traveling	taking	visiting
staying	working	baby-sitting	studying

```
I  T  A  K  I  N  G  N  R  G  N  I  S  I  I
B  C  A  M  P  I  N  G  S  N  N  S  I  N  I
B  A  I  A  S  I  I  I  T  L  I  T  Y  B  Z
T  E  H  C  A  T  A  D  A  A  I  A  A  B  I
R  A  F  I  A  L  A  I  Y  C  I  K  A  S  L
A  W  L  A  I  I  O  A  I  A  E  I  B  T  M
V  B  F  I  W  P  B  E  N  G  L  N  A  U  I
E  W  O  R  K  I  N  G  G  I  C  G  I  D  A
L  C  L  E  S  T  O  N  S  W  B  G  A  Y  I
I  B  I  C  N  N  P  S  V  N  S  I  B  I  N
N  B  A  B  Y  S  I  T  T  I  N  G  C  N  I
G  H  S  N  I  W  N  I  N  E  N  C  D  G  B
N  I  I  V  I  S  I  T  I  N  G  B  I  I  B
N  I  C  N  I  B  O  B  H  N  Q  I  S  I  N
```

1. ___camping___ in the mountains
2. _____ my uncle
3. _____ with my friends
4. _____ abroad
5. _____ tennis lessons
6. _____ at a restaurant
7. _____ my little cousin
8. _____ home

2 **Fill in the blanks with words from the box. Then answer the questions. Use information that is true for you.**

| coming |
| doing |
| going |
| anything |
| are |
| taking |

1. What are you ___doing___ next Friday night?_____
2. Are you doing _____ in the fall?_____
3. Are your classmates _____ lessons this summer?_____
4. When are your parents _____ on their next trip?_____
5. What _____ your friends doing this Saturday?_____
6. Is your favorite singer _____ to your city this year?_____

3 **Cross out ✗ the word that doesn't belong in each sentence. Then number the sentences to make a conversation.**

—— That is sounds fun. What are you studying?

—— When are you leaving in?

—— Cool! Are you studying in at the U.S.?

_1_ Hello, Patrick. What are you doing ✗ next summer?

—— I'm am studying abroad.

—— No, I'm not. I'm going in to England.

—— Are you going to the London?

—— I'm studying in English.

—— Yes, I am. It's is a really beautiful city.

4 What are these people doing this summer? Look at the pictures and write about them. Then make a suggestion for what they should do there. Use the words in the box or your own ideas.

| travel to Tokyo | take a swimming class | clean up before they leave | camping |
| take a break | see a museum exhibit | rest after class | work |

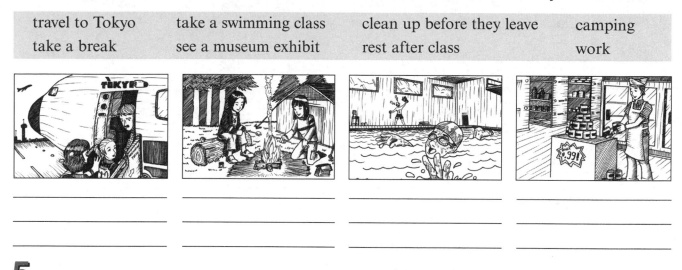

_____ _____ _____ _____

_____ _____ _____ _____

_____ _____ _____ _____

5 Read about what these people are doing this summer and fill in the blanks. Then complete the chart.

| this | for | too | on | in | from | is | she's | in | it's | at | he's | to | at |

Rose is _____ New York City. She's traveling ____ summer. First, she's visiting her friends _____ Mexico. She's leaving _____ June 16th. Then, _____ July, she's studying French abroad. She's studying ___ a French school in Lyon. ____ a little nervous, but she thinks ____ an exciting chance.

Robert is from Paris, France. He isn't going away this summer. He's staying home and baby-sitting his two cousins ____ two weeks. He's also working ____ a CD store and taking guitar lessons, _____. _____ a very good guitar player. He wants ____ be in a rock band. He thinks rock music ____ awesome!

	Rose	Robert	Me	My friend
baby-sitting				
staying home				
studying abroad	✓			
traveling				
taking music lessons				
visiting someone				
working				

6 Now complete the chart for you and a friend. Write about your summer plans.

_____

_____

_____

_____

LESSON B I'm having lunch with friends.

7 Fill in the blanks. Then write the questions.

1. Q: _____
   A: I'm meeting friends for lunch _____ 12:00 to 1:30.

2. Q: _____
   A: We're leaving _____ two days.

3. Q: _____
   A: She's having her hair done _____ two hours this afternoon.

4. Q: _____
   A: They're going to Korea _____ two weeks _____ July.

5. Q: _____
   A: I'm getting a check-up _____ 1:20 to 2:00 today.

8 Maria is going on vacation. Read her schedule and write about the things she has to do before she leaves.

Things to do today	Things to do tomorrow
9:00 a.m. check-up with Dr. Alden	7:00 a.m. get up early and go to dance class!
11:30 a.m. hair appointment at Beautz	8:00 a.m. clean room
1:00 p.m. lunch with Marco	9:00 a.m. meet Katie at Ricki's house
2:30-5:00 shopping! Buy Italian book, new shoes, electronic organizer, and camera	10:00 a.m. Leave for Italy!!!

_____

_____

_____

_____

_____

9 What do you usually have to do before vacation? Make a list, then write about it.

_____

_____

_____

_____

_____

Go for it!
Travel plans

Skim the travel schedule and answer the questions.

Australia Tours

Day	Class Events
Monday August 21st	Arrive at 9:00 a.m. in Sydney, Australia. Go to the Seaview Hotel and relax at the hotel pool. Lunch at the hotel. Surfing at Bondi Beach at 2:00 p.m.! Fish barbecue at 6:00 p.m. Evening free.
Tuesday August 22nd	Morning free. Lunch at the beach at 12:00. Visit Brett Whitely Art Museum at 2:30 p.m. Dinner at the Sydney Opera House restaurant at 6:00 p.m. Classical music concert at 8:00 p.m.
Wednesday August 23rd	Visit the kangaroos at the Sydney Zoo at 10:00 a.m.! Visit Powerhouse Museum at 2:00 p.m. See antique clock exhibit. Evening free.
Thursday August 24th	Visit the Ken Done Art Gallery at 10:00 a.m. Lunch at Red Restaurant at 12:00. Explore old Sydney at 2:00 p.m. Listen to a talk about food plants in the Botanical Gardens at 7:15 p.m.
Friday August 25th	Visit a guitar-maker's workshop at 10:00 a.m. Take guitar-making lesson. Visit the Australian Museum at 2:00 p.m. Guitar concert at 7:00 p.m.
Saturday August 26th	Morning free. Visit the Sydney Aquarium and see sharks at 2:00 p.m.! Beach party at 8:00 p.m.
Sunday August 27th	Breakfast at hotel at 6:00 a.m. Leave Sydney at 10:30 a.m.

1. How many museums does the class visit? _____

2. Where does the class learn about clocks? _____

3. What days does the class go to concerts? _____

4. How many art galleries does the class visit? _____

5. How many days does the class stay in Sydney? _____

What would you like to see in Australia? Make your own travel plans and write about them below. Use the information in the schedule above or your own ideas.

_____

_____

_____

_____

_____

Unit 15 LESSON A
How do you get to school?

1 Fill in the blanks. Then write how often you do these things.

1. We never __take__ the subway.

              I take the subway once a month.

2. I _____ my bike to the park on Saturdays.

              _____

3. We _____ the train to the city on weekends.

              _____

4. They always _____ the bus to go out.

              _____

5. My friend usually _____ home from school.

              _____

6. Our teacher _____ a taxi three or four times a week.

              _____

7. My sister _____ her car to school all the time.

              _____

8. I _____ a ride with my parents to school on rainy days.

              _____

2 How do these people get around? Look at the pictures and write sentences.

 30 min.

 15 min.

 10 min.

 1 hr.

She rides her bike
to guitar practice.
It takes about
thirty minutes

_____ _____ _____
_____ _____ _____
_____ _____ _____
_____ _____ _____

3 Unscramble the sentences. Then rewrite them to make a conversation. Remember to add punctuation.

___ parent's she my no drives car

A: _Masako, do you drive to school?_

___ sister with ride get my usually I a

B: _____

___ twenty takes about minutes it

B: _____

_1_ Masako drive do to you school

A: _____

___ car does how it take by long

B: _____

___ a have no, I don't car

A: _____

___ she does drive car her

B: _____

4 Change or cross out one word to make the sentences correct. Then write the questions.

1. Q: _How does your mom get to work?_

   A: My mom ta~~k~~e a bus to work. _takes_

2. Q: _____

   A: It takes me about twenty-five meters. _____

3. Q: _____

   A: No, we don't. We don't have a subway at our city. _____

4. Q: _____

   A: It's about two kilometers to the near hospital. _____

5. Q: _____

   A. No, she doesn't. My cousin doesn't have a car. She walks to a school. _____

5 Read about Amy's family and circle the transportation words. Then fill in the chart.

Message

| Accept | Reply | Forward | Delete | Print | Move to |

From: _____   Attachments:

To: _____

Copy: _____

Subject: _____

Hi, Sue.

Our family gets around town in a lot of different ways. I have a cool bike, so I usually ride my bike to school in the fall and spring. It's about three kilometers, so it takes about twenty minutes. My dad always drives to work, so I catch a ride with him in the winter. It's too cold and snowy to ride my bike then! My brother Brent usually takes the subway to work. He works in the city, so it takes about an hour. Mom doesn't like the subway and she can't drive, so she usually takes the bus to the store. It only takes five minutes.

Amy

Name	How they usually get around	How far they go	How long it takes
Amy			
Brent			
Mom			
Dad			

6 Write information about two people you know.

Name	How they usually get around	How far they go	How long it takes

LESSON B Take the Number 6 bus.

7 Unscramble the underlined words. Write the sentences.

1. I take the <u>narit.</u>   <u>I take the train.</u>
2. I ride my <u>kibe.</u>   _____
3. I <u>klaw.</u>   _____
4. I <u>kate</u> the bus.   _____
5. I take the <u>wubsay.</u>   _____

8 Read the telephone conversation. Then write notes on how to get to Ted's house.

Take the subway...

Zia: Ted, how do I get to your house?

Ted: Take the subway to the third subway stop.

Zia: Okay. Is your house near the subway stop?

Ted: No, then get on a Number 15 bus from the bus terminal. At the third stop, change buses and take the Number 23 for three stops till you get to the mall.

Zia: That's a long way! Is your house next to the mall?

Ted: No, it isn't. You have to walk. It's about eight blocks past the mall.

9 Circle the correct word.

1. Change trains at the East ((train)/ trains) station.
2. Where do I get (on / off) the Pine Street bus?
3. Change subways at the fifth subway (stop /go).
4. Can I get (on / to) the Green Street bus at the bus terminal?
5. Near the last subway (stop / start) you can find the shopping mall.

10 Write about how to get from your home to a favorite place. Give clear directions.

_____

_____

Scan the article and underline all the words to do with travel.

Going to work

Some people take helicopters to work!

People go to work in many different ways. Most people take some kind of public transportation.

Some people don't take a trip to work at all. They work at home. But most people around the world take a trip to work. In the *travel to work* pyramid, some people walk to work or ride a bike. A bike is very cheap and strong. With the materials in one car, you can make 200 bikes.

At the next level, there are fewer people. These people use public transportation. Buses are most popular but people also take boats, subways, and trains.

At the top of the pyramid, the fewest people own their own motorcycles or cars. Many of these people could take public transportation like buses or subways, but they prefer to travel by themselves.

11 **Read the article again about how people go to work and fill in the travel to work pyramid.**

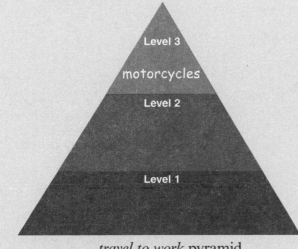

Level 3

motorcycles

Level 2

Level 1

travel to work pyramid

12 **What other ways do people travel to work? Write a list.**

1. _____
2. _____
3. _____
4. _____

Unit 16 LESSON A
Would you like to come to my party?

1 Complete the clues and fill in the crossword.

Down

1. S_____ I'm late.
3. I have an a_____ with the doctor tomorrow.
4. The school _____ is really interesting.

Across

2. My parents are going out. They asked me to b_____.
5. I l_____ pizza with ham and pineapple topping.
6. I enjoy v_____ museums.
7. Would you like to come to the rock c_____ on Friday?

2 (Circle) the correct word.

1. I have to finish my (date / (project)) on Sunday night.
2. They have to (baby-sit / baby-sitting).
3. Sorry, we can't (go / going) to the concert tomorrow.
4. She's sick and has a doctor's (date / appointment).
5. I'd love to but I (can / can't) have lunch with you today.

3 Number the sentences to make a conversation.

____ But I have to finish my project.

____ But what?

____ Friday night? I'd really like to, but . . .

____ It's my science project. Science is your favorite class, isn't it?

_1_ Julie, would you like to come to my party on Friday night? We're making pizza.

____ Sure! Can you help me?

____ Too bad. What project do you have to finish?

____ Yes, it is. Do you want some help with your science project?

____ Yes, come over after school on Friday.

4 Why can't these people go out? Look at the pictures and write their excuses.

1. (Saturday)   I'm sorry, I have to baby-sit on Saturday. _____
2. (next week)   _____
3. (Monday afternoon)   _____
4. (Sunday night)   _____
5. (Wednesday to Saturday)   _____

5 Unscramble these sentences.

1. you do have Saturday date on a night? _____
2. love I'd go to to dance the yes. _____
3. appointment have really I'd like to to the park but go I a doctor's. _____
4. are you your sure would brother to love skiing go? _____
5. weekend can come you to this dinner? _____

6 Read Elaine's notes and fill in her weekend schedule.

- Baby-sit Jennifer 7-10 p.m. Fri,
- Band practice -- Sun morn. 11-12.
- Doctor's appointment 575 Main Street, Room 239, Fri 3:00 p.m.

- Geography project - Patrick - Sat night?! See a movie?

- History homework with Rachel, Sun 7:00 p.m.
- Sat morning Tennis lesson 9:15
- Science test at 10:00, Friday morning
- Sun 2:00! Band concert, City Hall Theater. Wear black dress.

	Friday
Morning	Science test at 10:00!
Afternoon	
Night	

	Saturday
Morning	
Afternoon	
Night	

	Sunday
Morning	
Afternoon	
Night	

LESSON B **I have a doctor's appointment.**

7 Separate the words and punctuate to make sentences.

1. whoishavingthepicniconSaturday   Who is having the picnic on Saturday? _____

2. whatkindofnewfashionshowisit   _____

3. whenonFridayisthetalentshow   _____

4. whereisthenextsoftballgame   _____

5. whocangotothecostumecontest   _____

8 Use the words in the parentheses to write sentences.

1. (when / band concert)   When is the band concert? _____

2. (who / car race Saturday)   _____

3. (where / dance Friday)   _____

4. (who / having fashion show)   _____

5. (when / John costume party)   _____

9 Write about your weekend. What do you <u>want</u> to do? What do you <u>have</u> to do?

Go for it!
Notes and messages

Skim the notices on the camp bulletin board. Circle the ones that make an invitation, underline those that accept an invitation.

Confoundus Computer Camp Bulletin Board

Welcome to water skiing. Everyone can come to the beach at 3:30.

We're now having the campfire party on Wednesday night. Dress as your favorite alien.

Ever tried mountain climbing?

Now's your chance.

Meet Susan at 9 a.m. sharp on Friday.

Jack, sorry, I can't meet you at lunch. Maybe next week. Dora

Dan, thanks for the invitation. Yes, I'll come to the canoe race.

Jean

The teacher has a stomachache.

No Arts and Crafts class today.

Sailing lessons will be Thursday after dinner, not Wednesday.

Class full.

Read the messages and answer the following questions.

1. Who can't meet?_____

2. Why is there no Arts and Crafts class?_____

3. What is Jean going to do?_____

4. What is Susan teaching?_____

5. Why do you think the sailing lessons changed days?_____

What other activities do people like to do at camp? Write a list and circle the ones you like.

_____

_____

_____

_____

Review 4

1 Write the missing words in the blanks in the crossword.

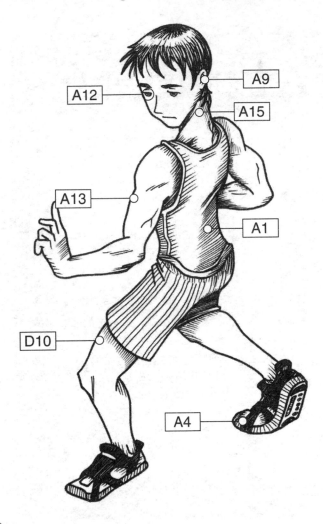

Down

2. I have a doctor's _____ at 3:00.
3. Let's play a _____ game.
5. You can change buses at the bus _____.
7. My school band has a _____ next week.
8. Saturday and Sunday are the _____.

Across

6. Let's have a _____ on the beach.
11. I think our English teacher is very _____.
14. Sheila has a _____ with a new friend.

2 Unscramble the sentences.

1. train meet let's the at after station concert the. _____

2. new should I a at job video a store get game. _____

3. listen didn't her to and she parents to go hospital the. _____

4. our talk to to about friends magazines fashion like we. _____

5. weekend you are going hang to at out this home? _____

3 (Circle) the correct word.

1. When are you (coming / come) back to the costume party?

2. Are you teaching music after the (band / concert)?

3. Is your friend working at the (train / party) station this summer?

4. When is the subway leaving for the next (stop / go)?

5. What is the band (going / doing) on Friday afternoon?

4 What's wrong with these pictures?

_____   _____   _____

_____   _____   _____

5 Fill in the missing letters to spell a new word.

r	e	a	l	l	y		
				y	e		
b	a	b	y		i	t	
	f	a		h	i	o	n
		f		o	t		
p	i	c		i	c		
			o	r	r	y	

Now write three sentences using all the words.

_____

_____

6 Number the sentences to make a conversation.

___ Ah, yes. Four people in a taxi. That's a good idea.

_1_ Hello, Carol, would you like to go to a fashion show?

___ How many subway stops is it?

___ I don't have a car on Thursday. We could take a taxi.

___ It's on Thursday night at the Sparta Shopping Mall.

___ Let's go with three more friends!

___ Oh, it's about seven stops.

___ Seven stops? Could we drive there?

___ Sparta Shopping Mall? How do we get there?

___ Sure, I'd love to. When is it?

___ Taxis are expensive.

___ Well, we have to take a bus to the subway terminal, then take a subway.

7 Look at the letters in appointment. How many other words can you make with these letters?

_____

_____

_____

My reading journal 2

Circle the correct word or phrase in each group.

Big Cat Adventure (Part 2)

I read a story called Big Cat Adventure. It was a very (exciting / long / sad) story. In the middle of the story, Yoshi and Tessie are in a cage with two (bicycles / policemen / pumas). When the bad people open the doors their boss sees Yoshi's (grandmother /foot /car). Later, Tessie controls the car to bring Yoshi a (knife / candy bar / helicopter). At the end of the story there is a helicopter with a lot of (policemen / pumas / candy bars) as well as Doctor Villaran and Professor Gatti. Finally he doctor invites Tessie and Yoshi (to have a cup of tea / to play football / to visit the puma hospital).

Match the phrases from each column to make sentences about the people (and animals!) in the story.

Yoshi	has long teeth	and then called his friend for extra help.
Tessie	saw Yoshi in the cage with the pumas	and drove to the harbor very quickly.
Doctor Villaran	was a good driver	and he bit the bad boss.
Professor Gatti	had an angry conversation with the bad boss	but he didn't see Tessie!
The bad boss	is an intelligent girl	but was very happy to watch her baby fight
Koko	drove with the Professor	and got a helicopter to help his friend.
Teo	is the head of the police	and helped Yoshi escape.
José	was very sleepy	and then he used a knife to escape.

What do you think?

1. Tessie and Yoshi were crazy to go onto the boat.
2. We buy and sell dogs. We can buy and sell pumas. The bad guys were not bad.
3. Would you like to work in a puma hospital? Why? Why not?

Self check 2

1 Now I can say . . . **Write the questions for these answers.**

Yes, I saw the new museum exhibit yesterday.

No, I can't stand his sunglasses.

No, we can't take the subway or the train.

I'd love to, but I have a date.

I get a ride with my friend to the band concert practice.

2 Now I can talk about . . . **Check the boxes and write an example.**

☐ things I like to buy and do _____

☐ body parts _____

☐ rules _____

☐ healthy foods and exercise _____

☐ fun activities and transportation _____

3 Now I can list . . . **Fill in the mind map with words about healthy habits.**

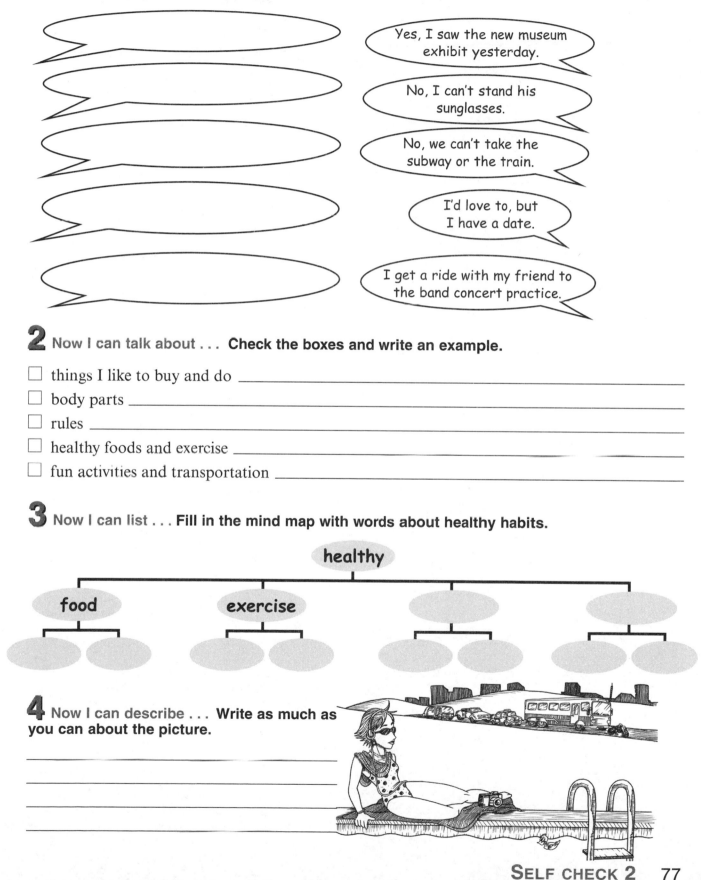

healthy

food   exercise

4 Now I can describe . . . **Write as much as you can about the picture.**

_____

_____

_____